Those Were the Times

Stories by Jack Foley

Those Were the Times

Those Were the Times: Stories by Jack Foley

Copyright © 2012 by Jack Foley
Copy Edit by Michael Ray King
Interior art by Sandy Haddock
Interior art on pages 20 and 44 by Tahtijana Owens
Cover design and layout by Ivy N. King
Back Cover Photograph by Wesley Foley
Interior layout and pagination by Jeff Swesky
Front cover art by Sandy Haddock
Typing by Becky Tyson
Final Edit by Beth Foley

Jack Foley
Those Were the Times: Stories by Jack Foley
160p. 7ill. cm.
ISBN 978-1-935795-09-4 softcover 978-1-935795-10-0 Kindle
1. Biography
2. Wit and Humor
Library of Congress Control Number: 2012946970

All Rights Reserved. No part of this book may be reproduced, stored in a retrieval system, or transmitted in any form or by any means, electronic, mechanical, photocopying, recording, or otherwise, without permission in writing from ClearView Press, Inc.

ClearView Press, Inc.
PO Box 353431
Palm Coast, FL 32135-3431
www.clearviewpressinc.com

Printed in the United States of America

Stories by Jack Foley

In loving memory of family and friends while growing up in Greater Gulf Hammock

Those Were the Times

Stories by Jack Foley

Table of Contents

The Flashback: Remember That Time?	vvi
Introduction: From Cotton Fields to Paradise	xi
Greater Gulf Hammock: Unmatched Natural Beauty	xiii
1 - Run For Your Life!	1
2 - Easy Money	7
3 - The Surprise at Sand Slough	21
4 - Wild Hogs and Catch Dogs	31
5 - Jumper Totin' Skinners, Blank Saturdays, and Juke Joints	43
6 - The Runaways	55
7 - Humor and Tragedy	71
8 - Frolics and Revivals	79
9 - A Chance to Win Provides "Hope!"	93
10 - Strange Things Actually Do Happen!	99
11 - The Last Days of the Hermits	107
12 - Believe It or Not, It's True!	113
13 - The Company Doctor	115
14 - Excitement at Cedar Key!	119
15 - A Short Story—The Long Hot Days	129
16 - The Dreaded Wash Day for Clothes	133
17 - The Last Chapter	137
About the Author	143

Those Were the Times

Stories by Jack Foley

The Flashback
Remember That Time?

The first warnings were frightening. An extremely dangerous typhoon named Marge was churning its way toward the coastal area of Korea, and we were in the projected path.

I was serving as a gunner's mate aboard the U.S.S. Toledo CA133, a heavy cruiser. We provided ground fire support for the 8th Army Command troops who were engaged in combat with the enemy.

The Fleet Admiral ordered a ceasefire for all naval ships and to immediately set a course to avoid the typhoon. The latest news was that Marge had now exceeded 150 mile per hour winds with dark, ominous clouds and heavy rains. The entire crew immediately prepared the ship for rough seas.

With gun mount secured, I made my way up to the bridge. It was close to the time to serve my three hour watch as one of the ship's phone talkers. The phone talkers were stationed at different locations on the ship forming an effective communications network with the ship's navigator. The bridge was the highest manned structure on the ship and provided a fantastic view of the entire horizon. When the seas got rough, there were a lot of pitching and rolling motions. These motions can get rough, and some phone talkers become sick. With Marge approaching these types of motions, pitch and roll could become incredibly bad.

When I arrived on the bridge, the phone talker I relieved was ever glad to see me. The sea was getting rough, dark clouds were moving in, and a slight rain had started. He was anxious to get off the bridge and go below deck.

All phone talkers were surprised when a young officer took over as navigator. It was a shock! Everyone expected to hear Commander Scarborough. Regarded as a harsh, unfriendly loner, the Commander also proved a superior talent as a navigator. Commander Scarborough spent most of his time observing and training younger navigators. He was always in charge where there were special situations, and this was an exceptionally special one. Typhoon Marge was an extremely dangerous typhoon.

The bridge phone talker relays the navigator's messages to the phone talkers and relays phone talkers' messages to the navigator. No other navigator but Commander Scarborough wore a set of phone talker phones. He heard all incoming and outgoing messages. He came across very harsh with any phone talker who did not perform to his high expectations. Commander Scarborough expected the bridge's phone talker to relay all messages to him "properly and accurately." I served with him on the bridge a number of times in special situations, but none could compare to this dangerous situation.

Commander Scarborough took charge. He told me to relay the message to all phone talkers that "He was in charge!"

"Seaman Foley," grumped Commander Scarborough. "Do you think you can perform your duties in some rough seas?"

"Yes, sir," I replied quickly. His statement surprised me because he called me by my name, Foley. Seaman, however, stuck as my name for the rest of the shift.

"You had sure as hell better be right," the Commander replied. "I can offer a worse choice."

For the first time, I carefully observed the features of the Commander. He towered just over six feet tall with the build of an athlete. His sun burnt bronze face held deep furrows like the face of a lifetime fisherman. He owned steel gray eyes, and he reminded me of some of the tough Cedar Key fishermen I knew.

"Sir," I replied carefully. "My three hour watch is almost over. My relief should be making his way to the bridge. Maybe I'll miss your 'worse' choice."

The Commander's response consisted of a long, hard look which ended with a shocking reply. "Your relief is not coming." He paused to let that sink in. "I have called all gunnery divisions and arranged for all phone talkers to remain on duty until the current danger ends. Your worse choice remains an option." The Commander, with those steel eyes fixed on me, actually smiled. What a shock. For a moment, I almost forgot about Marge! No one would ever believe me if I told of this event. "Commander Scarborough smiled!"

The seas grew rougher, and the hours to come felt like a lifetime of facing death.

The ship soon pitched and rolled in the turbulent, foaming waters. Swells raised the ship unbelievably high, and then the ship would suddenly shudder and crash down into the sea. With each huge swell, each drop felt like our last. Hard, angry winds from purple swirling clouds were as fierce as the seas.

At one point, we crashed down into a trough, and the bow of the ship went under water up to the eight inch gun turret. This seemed like the end! However, the bow popped out of the sea, and threw thousands of gallons of water over the ship. We had moved to a protected area off the bridge. Phone talker messages flew in from all locations. I could hardly relay them to the Commander and relay his messages back to the phone talkers. My voice choked with fear. I had never known fear this strong. I made every effort to control the fear by focusing on my phone talker duties. I tried, as much as possible, to ignore the thoughts of a fatal outcome.

I'm not sure how long our dangerous situation lasted. I know that as the seas calmed, I thought of growing up in Gulf Hammock and how I loved the summers. I looked forward to the last day of the school year and the first day of summer.

The seas calmed even more, the rains stopped, and the sun roared from its clouded hiding place. Everyone on the ship's crew cheered! I was relieved of my phone talker duty and I made my way below deck.

Stories by Jack Foley

Introduction

From Cotton Fields to Paradise

Have you ever picked cotton? It's a dern bad job! The sun gets hot early and that clay dirt between rows is hot on your bare feet. I have some shoes, but they also hurt my feet, and that's not all! The cotton bolls have thorns around the outer edge, and they stick in your hand as you pick the cotton out of the boll. That hurts! Do you wonder who is telling you this and why I'm in this hot cotton field?

I'll tell you anyway!

My daddy was workin' for a large lumber mill here in South Alabama near the town of Florala. The mill is closin' soon. My daddy has accepted a job at another large lumber mill in Florida at a small town called Gulf Hammock. The problem of it is that a mill house is not available, and we have to wait here 'til one is available.

He is there, and we are in the middle of a hot cotton field. Here is my mother! Here is my older brother, Fred, older sister, Doris, then Betty, then Don.

My name is Jack. I'm six years old and that is why I'm here in this hot cotton field. My mother got us this job pickin' cotton because we need to buy food while he is gone. She says "the entire nation is in a depression and there ain't hardly any jobs. Your daddy is looking to get a job. We have to do the best we can."

I started thinkin' more about mother and the other children and decided I'd think less of my problems and stop complainin' out loud.

Four days passed and even though I thought I still had things to complain out loud about, I did not. I picked more cotton than usual those days. Then on the fifth day, in the early afternoon, I couldn't believe what I saw. It was real. I shouted, "It's here! I see it! It's come for us!" I threw my cotton sack down and started running toward a large flatbed Model B truck. It was movin' slowly alongside of the cotton field.

Mother was close to me, and she hollered at me to "Stop! Right now!" I stopped. She told me to get my cotton sack and meet at the back of the cotton field. Each of us turned in our cotton and was paid. I was paid $1.00. It was my best pay day, and I gave it all, but enough to buy some candy, to mother.

The truck was loaded late that evening. We were ready to leave for the little town in Florida called "Gulf Hammock."

It was early afternoon the next day when we were told by the driver that we were not far from Gulf Hammock. The road became very narrow. There was barely room for the truck. It looked like we were drivin' through a jungle. It was my first view of Gulf Hammock and nothin' like I had ever seen. It was beautiful! The view would become a lasting impression.

We began to cross over some small bridges. There were crystal clear creeks flowing under each bridge.

I saw some fish darting from under scattered patches of lily pads. I could'n hardly wait to get off the truck and start explorin'!

We turned off the main road across from a large building that was the commissary store. We drove a short distance, and the driver parked in front of a large white, two-story building. It was the boarding house for mill workers.

It was Saturday afternoon, and I saw my father sitting on the porch. He was waiting for us. It was a reunion I will never forget. We drove to our mill house, and my new life in Gulf Hammock began.

Stories by Jack Foley

Greater Gulf Hammock
Unmatched Natural Beauty

The region called Greater Gulf Hammock is located between the Withlacoochee River to the south, the Suwannee River to the north, and bound to the west by the Gulf of Mexico. This region contains thousands of acres of land which include sand hills, dry hammocks, cypress heads, bay heads, wet hammocks, swamps, and marsh islands. There are many backwater tidal creeks that snake their way from the Gulf up through marsh grass and around small marsh grass islands of cedar trees, cabbage palms, Spanish bayonets, and other assorted growth. The creeks often end in wet hammocks or large flats of mud and marsh grass. The continuous flow of incoming and outgoing tides bring in an abundance of fish and attracts all sorts of wildlife.

The Greater Gulf Hammock region was originally inhabited by the Timucuan Indians. There are numerous sites where there were once villages. Consequently, Indian artifacts were once abundant over the entire region but due to current interest, they are becoming scarce.

Negro slaves that were freed at the end of the Civil War were the early settlers of Greater Gulf Hammock. Some of these slaves were freed from a place called the Plantation. The Plantation was located a few miles south of the town of Gulf Hammock. For a few years, the name of the town of Gulf Hammock was changed to Gunn Town and then later back to Gulf Hammock.

The Greater Gulf Hammock region was of great interest to hunters, fishermen, loggers, turpentine workers, fugitives, roving preachers, loners, pioneer farmers, a few remaining Indians, and some wandering gypsies who were anxious to bless your money which was often limited.

This may be considered a minor downside, as the region was blessed with every sort of stinging or biting insect known to humans. This included mosquitoes, yellow flies, horse flies, mule flies, sand gnats, yellow jackets, ticks, redbugs, hornets, wasps of all sorts, and spiders. Mix all of these in with cottonmouth moccasins, rattlesnakes, coral snakes, alligators, and a damp freezing cold in the winter and you can begin to see a minor inconvenience with living in such a beautiful environment! Oh yes, I forgot to mention the size and number of cockroaches! Every human dwelling had these as constant co-dwellers along with other unwanted guests.

In 1926, a large lumber mill was built in the town of Gulf Hammock by Groves Dowling Lumber Company. The lumber mill built a large commissary store that included the company offices and the post office. The commissary also contained a dry goods section, groceries, meat market, pharmacy, and a section for ice cream, drinks, candy, guns, fishing tackle, and other assorted items for your every need. This was where the company got back almost, if not all, the balance of a worker's pay. More details about that later! There was also a small clinic with a doctor and a nurse, a school house (that also served as a church and a barber shop), a garage, a gas station, a 50 room, two-story hotel, and a boarding house.

The white housing was mostly located on two parallel streets with frame houses on each side of the street facing each other. Many were the typical southern shot gun design or slightly modified. The houses usually had two or three bedrooms. The company took rent out of a worker's pay every two weeks. The houses had indoor facilities. However, the water was so bad (iron and sulfur), that all facilities turned orange. The houses were wired for lights with bare light sockets hanging from the ceiling on electric cords. However, the lights went off in the evening when the mill shut down and didn't come on until almost 5:00 a.m. when the mill started up. There was no heat except a small fireplace in the front room. With a roaring fire, the heat only reached out a few feet. You could stand in front of the fireplace and roast on one side and freeze on the other. The houses had no insulation. Most everyone cooked on a wood stove.

The Negro housing was located in six different quarters, referred to by most whites as the "Negro quarters." Two of the quarters had juke joints, and they were larger than the regular small frame houses. I'll share more about the jukes later in the story. The quarters' houses were small, frame buildings with no indoor facilities, no water, no insulation, and usually had a small wood heater. There were outhouses and a water faucet or hand pump for each of the quarters.

To provide labor for the lumber mill operations, the owners or managers would often send out individuals to round up workers from other mill areas including Florida, Alabama, Georgia, Mississippi, and South Carolina. Initial pay for labor was around a dollar a day for a ten-hour day and out of this came rent for housing and a doctor fee. Workers could draw a little money for groceries at the commissary store up to what they had earned. This was usually on Tuesday or Thursday afternoon and was called draw days. The company got back most (and sometimes) all the money a worker earned.

There were about 600 hundred workers at the mill when we moved there. That included the logging operation, the saw mill, planer mill, dry kilns, lumber yard, commissary store, maintenance shops, and other assorted jobs. The lumber company owned close to 130,000 acres of timber land along the Gulf of Mexico.

There were some folks living in the area who didn't work for the lumber mill—a few farmers, folks who lived off the land, and some I don't know for sure what they did for a living. There were three stores that had private owners. One store was located a couple of miles north of Gulf Hammock where the Waccassaa River crosses Highway 19/98. The old building is still there. Peeks Store was almost a half-mile south of Gulf Hammock on Highway 19/98, and Gavins Store was on 19/98 about a half-mile south of Peeks Store. These buildings are no longer there. Driving through Gulf Hammock today on Highway 19/98, there is one of the old logging trains beside the highway.

This brings me to the beginning of my story. My family has now lived in Gulf Hammock for six years. This is the last day of school, and I am finishing the seventh grade. In addition to the stories I will share, I will acquaint you with information about the Greater Gulf Hammock region.

The Author's Historic Note

A great event happened in 1926. It led to the building of most of the town of Gulf Hammock.

One of the largest lumber mills in the south moved from Odessa, Florida, to Gulf Hammock. The owners of the mill were Dr. E. W. Groves and two Dowling brothers. They built "train" roads and used trains to transport logs from the logging woods to the lumber mill. They purchased 132,000 acres of timber land. One of the trains used to transport logs is on display beside Highway 19/98 as you pass through Gulf Hammock.

The Author's Comment:

Look Quick!

Chapter 1

Run for Your Life!

There was one week of school left in the seventh grade before the beginnin' of summer, and I began to think how I met Nathan Curney the summer before.

Nathan lived close to Peek's Store, and I walked by his house once, or sometimes twice a week to get a cold drink. I enjoyed sittin' on the side porch of Peek's Store and visitin' with Mrs. Peek. She really seemed to like to visit. She told me lots about Nathan Curney before I met him and suggested I stop and visit with him. I decided if he was home, I would stop. Mrs. Peek seemed to have a high regard for Nathan Curney. I learned Nathan's father was three-quarters Seminole and one-quarter Negro. Mrs. Peek told me Nathan worked as a huntin' and fishin' guide for Mr. Peek and his friends. He also ran a trap line usin' about a hundred traps. Nathan sold all kind of game through Peek's Store and to lots of Negro customers. Mrs. Peek was tellin' me that when someone got lost in Gulf Hammock, it was not unusual for Nathan to be contacted to join in the search.

I left Peek's Store and stopped by Nathan's house. I saw him down at a small pond across from his house. A couple of gators, some raccoons, rabbits, possums, and other critters lay at Nathan's feet.

"Mr. Nathan," I greeted him. "My name is Jack Foley, and I been wantin' to stop by and say hello."

"Jack, I know who you are. You are Mr. Albert Foley's boy. What I want to know is if you know how to skin out a small alligator?"

"No, sir, but I do know how to skin out and clean squirrels, clean fish and frog legs," I replied with great pride.

"Well now," said Nathan with a smile. "That's a start. Now watch me dress out this raccoon and you practice on the other one."

That began a great friendship. Lookin' back in time, I remember all the stories Nathan told me about the United States Army, roundin' up Indians and takin' their land, and sendin' them out west. Many died along the way.

I told Nathan stories that my grandmother told me. Her great-grandmother was Creek Indian and she and her white husband owned a farm in South Alabama. They hid runaway Indians and slaves in a large hidden area dug out under the barn. When there was a new moon causin' a dark night, her husband would guide them into south Florida to join up with the Seminoles. They were still at war with the U.S. Army soldiers.

The more I learned how the U.S. Army treated Indians, the more I didn't like cowboys or U.S. soldiers and Indian picture shows. The Indians always lost.

Nathan insisted I not call him "Mr. Nathan." His good friends, old or young, called him "Nathan."

When other adults were around, I asked if I could call him Mr. Nathan, and he said, "No. Do you want me to call you Mr. Jack?"

"No, sir," I replied.

"Sir is okay," responded Nathan with a smile. "Now that the formalities are over, I do want to hear about those wrestlin' matches takin' place over to Aunt Liza's pump."

"Well," I responded thoughtfully. "Sometimes when I go by the pump I'm alone and at times Joe and Bull Berryhill are with me. That is some good water! It tastes just like that cool, clear water comin' out of Wekiva Springs. All the Gulf Hammock water in the mill houses is terrible. The water comin' outta the spigots in the mill houses turn everythin' brown and smells like sulfur mixed with rotten eggs."

Nathan smiled. "It is the best water in the Hammock. No, continue on about the wrestlin' matches."

"Well," I said, "The Negro boys choose one of us to wrestle one of them. If we win, we git a drink of water, and if they win, we git nothin'."

"Sounds fishy," said Nathan while laughin'.

"It's worse than fishy," responded Jack. "They don't know any rules. If their wrestler is losin', one or sometimes more of them will run up and kick our wrestler or maybe their wrestler will bite, stick their fingers in their eyes, or somethin' else not allowed. Most of the time, we leave without water."

The way Nathan was laughin', you could tell he was really amused.

When he stopped laughin', Nathan said "To be as fair as possible, you need a referee."

Jack responded quickly, "It would have to be one of them and the unfairness would continue."

"What about Franklin Schuler?" asked Nathan.

"I think he would be fair, but I doubt he would consider it. He is the strongest and by far their best wrestler. It would make it more fair for me or Joe to win," I responded.

"Jack, there is somethin' else I want to talk to you and Franklin about," said Nathan. "I hear Leonard Smallwood and some other folk are settin' up some boxin' matches on Saturday afternoons at Peek's Store. Gonna hafta pay a nickel to watch and bet on whose gonna win each fight. The winner of each fight gits paid a quarter, and the loser gits nothin'," said Nathan.

Nathan continued, "That's what Mr. Peek told me. Said it'll git a little more business for his store. What's the chance of you gettin' a match with Franklin Schuler? I think a match between a black and a white will draw a bigger crowd. There will be more blacks for sure. Mr. Peek will surely make more money,"

Nathan managed to schedule us two matches in the next two weeks. This gave him time to work with Franklin in order to be sure he knew some basic rules and had some skills. Nathan told me he was pleased that Franklin already had developed some skills and could follow some rules. There would be two, five round matches—the first and then the last match.

Neither Nathan, Franklin, nor I had no idea of the explosive situations these two boxin' matches would create.

To begin with, Nathan was right about one thing. It did draw a mixed crowd of both blacks and whites. Over half the small crowd, on their arrival, had already been hittin' the moonshine or some other form of intoxication. Even the law was there. Wild Cat Jones stood tall, all dressed out in his deputy uniform. Only eight weeks ago he got out of jail for moonshinin'. I liked Wildcat. Mr. C.D. Tummond joined me, Franklin, and Nathan. He refereed some of the boxin' matches. Mr. C.D. was employed as the Payroll Master for Patterson-McInnis Lumber Company—the largest lumber company in the south.

"Well," said C.D. to our little group with a big smile. "I think you've done it now. I suggest all of you run now!"

I replied, "Mr. C.D., I hope you will help work things out when this is over."

"Well, as a starter," said C.D. "Nathan can vanish into Greater Gulf Hammock like an Indian and stay until whatever happens here blows over. It's the rest of you that will feel the heat."

Leonard Smallwood began to organize the first bout. It was time for Franklin and me. The ring was marked off with white lines laid in a large square along the ground. If you stepped over this line, the fight ended and you lost. Franklin and I met in the center of the ring. C.D. explained the rules, and the fight was on. My brother, a good boxer, helped me develop a plan before the fight. Franklin had the reach on me with his long, strong arms.

I moved in close and used short, hard body punches. I could not allow him to land his hard punches to my head or body. Franklin tried to shove me off at arm's length. The fight became much like a wrestlin' match. The first three rounds ended. The crowd was gettin' louder and unhappy. I was tirin' at the end of round three. I knew if Franklin kept up his attack, I would possibly lose in round four.

At the start of round four, Franklin started his attack. He stepped on a small rock kicked up earlier durin' the fight. He twisted his ankle and dropped his guard. Franklin was fallin' as I hit him, and he went down. C.D declared the fight over and I was declared the winner.

The crowd went wild. A couple of fights broke out. Some of the crowd demanded we start our second fight now instead of waitin' 'til all fights were over.

Wild Cat Jones broke up the two or three fights in the crowd. As most of the crowd now demanded the second fight, we were asked by C.D., Wild Cat Jones, and Leonard Smallwood to continue with the second fight. The fight did not last long. Franklin started by puttin' on an all-out, pressin' hard attack to win. Just when I thought I could counter his attack, I accidentally stepped out of the line drawn for the edge of the ring. C.D. stopped the fight and declared Franklin the winner. Several more fights broke out. I made a run to leave Peek's Store and git to the safety of the woods. I noticed Nathan, Franklin, C.D., and believe it or not, Wild Cat Jones slightly ahead of me.

The fight made the owners of the mill really mad. They vowed such boxing matches would not happen again—and they didn't! This was my and Franklin's last boxin' match in Gulf Hammock.

Those Were the Times

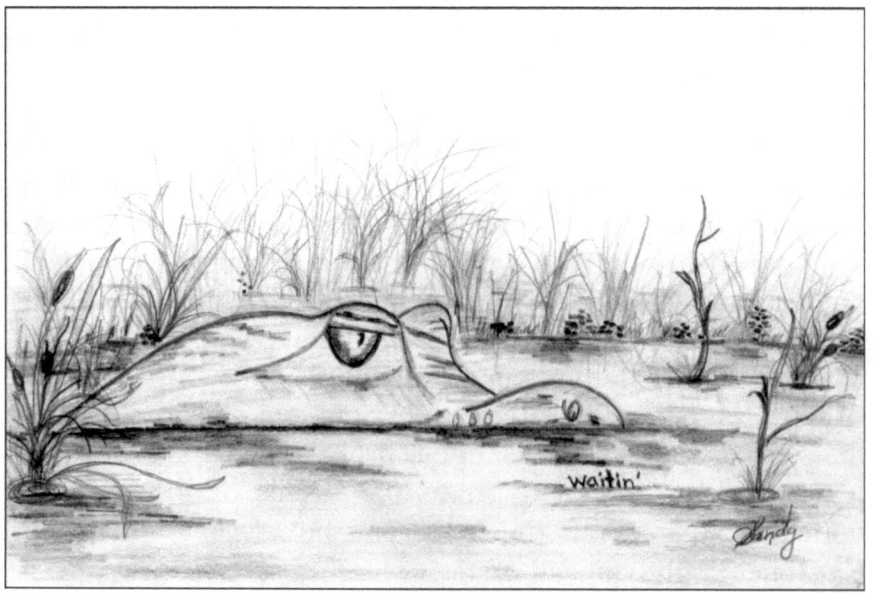

Chapter 2

Easy Money

There was absolute silence, and then the school bell rang out announcin' the beginnin' of summer. Thank God eighth grade was over! There was much excitement with kids hollerin', jumpin' around, and huggin' each other. Kids poured out windows and doors. A few minor fights broke out on the school grounds as old scores were settled without the danger of gettin' spanked by Principal Guy Smith. He had a big paddle named Sambo, and he didn't mind usin' it! Matter of fact, at times, I think he enjoyed usin' it. My friends, Joe and Bull and I were all in the principal's class as seventh graders. Joe this year, and Bull and I last year. Bull and I would be bussed over to Bronson, the county seat, to start high school the next year, and Joe would have to stay on in Gulf Hammock to complete the eighth grade. Joe was not pleased to be left a full year without Bull and me around.

The three of us went by my house before leavin' for Bull and Joe Berryhill's house. With Ma's okay, and that of Joe and Bull's parents, I moved in with the Berryhill family at the beginnin' of summer. They lived about three miles south of Gulf Hammock, just beyond Gavin's Store. Joe, Bull and I had agreed to cut and split two cords of wood each week. We'd sell part of the wood and the Berryhills would keep the rest. We'd get paid fifteen cents spendin' money for each cord we cut. We planned to start our wood cuttin' project on Monday, and on Friday evenin', our big plan was to gig frogs at Boggy Pond and at a nearby borrow pit. Little did we know that this night would lead to a big dream of easy money and one scary adventure—certainly one I'd never forget!

We had the gig, headlights, and croaker sacks for frogs ready to go just before dark when Mrs. Berryhill called out as we started out the front gate.

"You boys better be careful. You know Boggy Pond is full of moccasins and 'gators. And Bull, you make Joe and Jack mind!"

"Yes Ma'am," Bull replied. Out of her ear range Joe asked, "How come Ma puts you in charge since you ain't no smarter than me or Jack?"

"Well," replied Bull, "I may not be any smarter, but I'm a-goin' to make you mind, and if either of you don't think so, you'll be in big trouble with me and with Ma when we get back home. Besides, Ma is still mad at you and Jack for gettin' into a fight with our cousins the last time we were in Romeo. That's why they leave us home now when they visit Grandpa and Grandma Markham. Now I can't go either 'cause Ma says you two can't be trusted alone."

Joe didn't respond as we started down the narrow trail of the hammock through thick, rugged growth toward Boggy Pond. To me, there always was somethin' mysterious about the hammock, and the mystery intensified at night. Strange sounds and movements punctured the silence. Bull carried the gig and led the way with his headlight. Joe and I followed close behind with our headlights off in order to save batteries.

"Hey," said Joe who was close behind Bull. "Let me carry the gig, and I'll move you toward Boggy Pond a little faster." Bull shot back, "Why in the world don't you be quiet?"

As we came closer to Boggy Pond, we heard a chorus of big bull frogs and smaller frogs that were joined by a passel of crickets. Cicadas joined in. The air was filled with hammock music. It was excitin' just to listen!

"Them are some big rascals," stated Bull, "We might get enough frog legs tonight to make fifty cents each at Gavin's or Peek's Store."

"Ain't no way," I responded. "Ain't neither of them a-goin' to pay as much as fifty cents to each of us. Neither of them old bastards will pay what the frog legs are worth. They'll git 'em cheap as they can. They 'bout as bad as the Commissary Store for makin' every penny they can."

"I think the Commissary Store is the worst." Joe replied. "They try to git back most everythin' they pay the mill workers. The owners of the mill even make their own money. 'Member the time they paid the workers with that babbit money? They wanted to get back everythin' they pay workers."

"Ain't no way we could even sell them to the Commissary Store," I said. "They'd claim they even owned the frogs in the hammock or else pay us in babbit."

Bull interrupted, "We come out here after them frogs and not to bitch 'bout greedy people. Besides, both of you know it's better to keep your mouths shut and not go bad mouthin' the mill owners. Pa and Jack's Pa won't have no job. Too much mouthin' off just ain't tolerated."

"Whose gonna tell on us?" asked Joe. Nobody answered as we quietly moved closer to the edge of Boggy Pond. Both Joe and I turned our headlights on.

"Bull! Joe! Look what I got in my light," I said with a twinge of excitement. Bull and Joe looked toward my light where a large cottonmouth moccasin was in the process of tryin' to swallow a big bullfrog. The bullfrog was makin' a terrible chokin' noise—the sound of death.

"Bull, Joe said, "take that frog away from that damn snake."

"Take it away yourself," Bull responded.

Without further comment, the decision was made to allow the poisonous snake to carry on with its swallowin' efforts.

We carefully moved around the edges of Boggy Pond and ended up with about thirty bullfrogs. We could have got a lot more, but there were too many places where you just couldn't get to the edge of the water to gig. We did see a couple more moccasins and a few 'gators. None of the 'gators were very big.

"Let's go on to the bar pit and get a few more frogs. We'll build a fire to help keep the 'skeeters away and skin out the frog legs," said Bull.

Joe responded while slappin' at mosquitoes, "I don't think Jesus could keep the skeeters away much less a little fire."

"Joe," said Bull firmly, "Ma and Pa both have warned you 'bout makin' Jesus statements. If I tell them, they will beat your bony little ass."

"Bull," said Joe, "If my bony little ass was beat every time I'm threatened, I wouldn't have a bony little ass left. As a matter of fact, I wouldn't even be able to eat 'cause you need an ass for a bowel movement!"

I interrupted, "Let's forget Joe's bony little ass and head on to the bar pit. These 'skeeters git worse as the night wears on."

We continued through the woods until we came out into a large clearin' which contained the borrow pit. We heard some frogs, but nothin' like the chorus at Boggy Pond. We eased up to the edge of the water and turned on our headlights. Joe was usin' his light to search across the rather large body of water trapped in the borrow pit.

"Hey," said Joe. "Look what I see."

We all looked in the direction of Joe's light and were stunned at the size of two large, red eyes shinin' in the light. No doubt it was one huge 'gator. Alligators were a common sight, but this one was as big as any I'd ever seen.

"Quick," Bull said. "Turn off your lights and see if I can call that big scoundrel a little closer."

Bull made the sound of a baby 'gator. He would stop for a moment and then repeat the sounds. After about five minutes, Bull turned on his light. The 'gator had moved much closer. We could now get a good idea of his size. He was huge! Maybe twelve to fourteen feet long.

Bull was excited. "Listen, there's a fellow from Silver Springs that's lookin' for large, live 'gators. If we capture one alive as big as this one, he'll come by and pick him up and pay as much as five dollars a foot. That 'gator is worth maybe seventy dollars!"

This was more money than we could imagine. We were talkin' big money.

"We need a plan on how to capture that 'gator," said Bull with excitement.

Joe and I quickly agreed, and we began talkin' about how we might capture the 'gator. Bull would take care of reachin' the fellow at Silver Springs. I was the first to respond to the beginnin' of a plan.

"My daddy has a roll of small cable," I began. "Maybe it was a piece left over from the mill. He also has some large staples. We could cut a small hickory tree that's not too big 'round and make a noose. Do you think the three of us can hold a 'gator that big with a good catchpole?"

Bull picked up on this idea, "You could cut a hickory back of where you live. Make the pole 'bout ten or twelve feet long, then drive in large staples 'bout a foot apart and thread in the cable. We could make a noose at the end of the poll and surely hold him."

"I can already hear the talk all over Gulf Hammock," Joe sarcastically responded. "Three young idiots et by one large 'gator. For the sake of not bein' thought of as totally stupid, I think we should all swear to Jesus not to tell a livin' soul 'bout this crazy plan until we've got that 'gator tied to a tree and that fellow from Silver Springs is on the way over with our money."

"I can't see you swearin' to Jesus 'bout nothin'," replied Bull. "We'll just swear to keep our mouths shut which is somethin' that's gonna be hard for you two to do."

We all agreed to swear. The plan was in motion. Bull told his Ma that I needed to run home Saturday. He and Joe would come by my house early on Sunday, and I'd come back home with them. Mrs. Berryhill was a little puzzled and also curious. She asked, "What's so important that Jack has to run back home and that you both need to go and get him?"

Joe immediately replied, "We just wanted to stop by Peek's Store and get a Pepsi and maybe visit with Nathan Curney a spell. He knows where there are lots of bullfrogs and where we may get a better price than from Gavin's Store."

Bull and I listened with admiration. Joe could really make up stories and quick. Mrs. Berryhill looked at Joe intently and finally said it was okay but only if there wasn't more to Joe's story that could get us in trouble.

I left early Saturday mornin' and decided to stop by and talk to Nathan Curney—not about frogs, but about catchin' that large 'gator. Nathan smiled as he saw me comin' up the porch and said, "Hurry up and go get them Pepsi's." He threw me a dime, and I ran back to Peek's Store and returned with two Pepsi's.

"Nathan, I want to ask you 'bout how to catch a large 'gator, maybe close to fourteen foot."

Nathan quickly replied, "Shoot the big rascal first."

"We can't do that," I replied. "We can get big money for him if he's 'live. Joe, Bull and I plan to split maybe sixty or seventy dollars."

I carefully explained the plan to Nathan.

"Jack," said Nathan firmly, "Stay out of the water 'cause you boys are kinda' small for that size 'gator. Don't wrap that cable around your arm or body. That 'gator's gonna roll, sling that big tail, and raise mighty hell. You boys better be awful careful. I know you boys don't want to split up that big money four ways so I'll set back and wait for you to show up and buy us Pepsi's with all them riches you'll have."

We talked awhile about the fights at Peek's Store and about Franklin decidin' not to fight anymore. Matter of fact, he was tryin' to get a summer job at the mill. I told Nathan I'd get by to see Franklin before long. We talked awhile more and then I went on home.

Ma was surprised I was back so soon. She gave me a big hug as if I'd been gone a year. There were seven of us kids and life was tough for both Ma and Dad. However, Dad loved the hammock, and Ma always worked hard takin' care of the family, always hopin' for a better life. I asked about Dad, and Ma said she thought he was out in the garden. I went out back.

"Hey," he said when he saw me. "I thought you was workin' with the Berryhill boys."

"I am," I replied. "I just need a few things to make a catchpole."

When I explained to Dad what I was lookin' for, he thoughtfully asked, "Just why are you boys suddenly makin' a catchpole? I have a feelin' there's somethin' special somewhere out there that you think needs catchin'. Ya'll just be careful."

I told Dad, "We thought we'd carry it along with us and maybe catch pigs, small 'gators, or whatever we might find. Nathan Curney said it was a good idea to have a good catchpole around."

"Well," Dad said thoughtfully, "Knowin' you as I do, I'm not sure I'm hearin' it all."

I hoped I was not too specific and was pleased when Dad helped me gather up all I needed except the hickory pole. I knew he'd make me promise to let that big 'gator alone if he was aware of our plan.

That afternoon, I found the perfect hickory and cut the small tree down. It was about fourteen feet long and two and one-half inches in diameter. By nine o'clock that night, the staples were in, the cable was threaded with a noose on one end with at least seven extra feet on the opposite end. The plan was movin' ahead.

Bull and Joe showed up early Sunday mornin'. Ma hugged them both. They talked to Dad a few minutes, and we left for the Berryhill house. A short distance from home, we stopped for Bull and Joe to carefully examine the catchpole. It got a big okay, and we walked down the narrow hard-top road, crossed Nigger Bridge toward Peek's Boat Landing, and cut through the woods on a dirt trail by Aunt Liza's house to Peek's Store. Just before Peek's Store, we saw Nathan Curney sittin' on his front porch. He smiled as we approached. "Here come them 'gator catchin' rich folk. Gonna stop off and see how the po folks live?"

"Mr. Nathan," Bull said, "We'd like you to look over this catchpole Jack built and not tell a soul about this 'gator catchin' thing."

"Don't Mr. Nathan, me." Nathan replied. "I told you boys to call me Nathan. Sayin' Mr. Bull, Mr. Joe, and all that "Mr." stuff makes it sound like you're talkin' to someone more important than you are. I think everybody's the same importance. Some just got more stuff than others. Now, let's look at this fine catchpole."

Nathan carefully examined the catchpole. "Boys, the pole is green, and I don't know how good staples will hold in green wood. You might fix the cable at the end opposite the noose where it can't slide through 'cause that 'gator can snatch that cable straight through." Nathan thoughtfully looked at the three of us and then continued. "I done told Jack 'bout stayin' out of the water with dat 'gator and some other things. Come back when you're rich and I'll call you Mr. Bull, Mr. Joe, and Mr. Jack and hope you'll give this po folk a whole case of Pepsi's. Now be extra careful, and don't do nothin' stupid."

We stopped by Peek's Store for Pepsi's and then hid the catchpole just before we got back to the Berryhill house. We ate supper early, got our frog gig headlights, and started for the borrow pit. We were all three et up with excitement! The time had finally come.

We didn't speak 'til we came to the openin' for the borrow pit. We eased up to the edge of the water, all headlights off. It was black dark.

"Must be a new moon." Joe whispered. "Bull, just use your headlight to see if you can find that 'gator."

Bull's light streaked across the water of the borrow pit and wandered around, and suddenly there were the two large red eyes, not more than thirty feet from where we were standin'. Bull turned off his headlight.

"Call him closer." I whispered. I could feel my heart beatin' a little harder.

Bull made his baby 'gator sounds. Then he'd stop for a few seconds and call again. After about three or four minutes, he stopped and turned on his headlight. The 'gator had moved a little closer. He was now about twenty feet away and in water that was no deeper than three feet. Suddenly, the 'gator sank to the white sand bottom.

Joe whispered, "Let's ease out and get this noose around his neck. We'll be real close to the bank if we can't hold him and need to get out."

"Nathan told us to stay out of the water." I whispered. "What do you want to do, Bull?" I continued, my heart never havin' beat any faster or harder.

Bull thought for a minute and whispered back, "Joe, if you want to take the front of the pole and ease out toward the 'gator, Jack can take the middle part, and I'll take the end of the pole. I can hold that 'gator off the two of you."

"I notice you are the farthest from that 'gator and Jack and I are closest," Joe whispered back.

"Do you want to try or not?" asked Bull impatiently. "If you want to try, git yo butt on out there."

Joe slowly eased into the edge of the water. He had the front of the catchpole with 'bout four foot of the cable hangin' from the end of the catchpole to the top of the noose. Joe's light was on the 'gator now, and both Bull and I also had our lights on him. The 'gator could easily be seen on the white sand through the clear water. The water was not even four feet deep.

Joe eased out, takin' a slow slidin' step along the sand until he was about six or seven feet from the 'gator. The 'gator lay still. Joe eased the noose into the water and down to the edge of the 'gator's nose. The 'gator moved forward. His head and one leg were now in the noose. All of us were experiencin' a high level of excitement.

"Ready?" Joe whispered. We whispered back that we were ready. Bull pulled the catchpole back with all his might. Joe and I were holdin' on for dear life as we were almost snatched down by Bull.

The water exploded. The 'gator stripped all the staples from the catchpole. He rolled. He swung his huge tail in every direction. I no longer had a hold of the catchpole. I had lost all sense of direction not knowin' where the 'gator, Joe, Bull or the bank was. Stark fear came later. Now all I felt was panic. I had a glimpse of Bull goin' up the bank with his headlight still on. Frantically I tried to get to the bank. I fell down in the water twice before makin' it up the bank. Joe and Bull were already there. We all sat quietly in soakin' wet clothes. No one said a word for what seemed like a long time. It probably was not more than five minutes. Bull finally spoke "I ain't never seen nothin' like this where all hell done broke loose. Joe, are you and Jack okay?"

"I ain't never goin' to be the same again," I responded in a quiverin' voice. "I ain't never been so scared in my life. I think I even pissed in my pants but it's hard to tell."

Finally Joe spoke. "This was a damn good plan to get us all killed. I tried to tell you two at the beginnin' of this mess. I tell you what I got out of this. I got religion. I told Jesus to get me out of this and I'd never make another Jesus statement."

Bull suddenly was angry. "This ain't the end of this. We're gonna come back with a better plan. We're gonna catch that damn 'gator. I ain't scared of that son a bitch."

"I know," replied Joe. "I shore noticed you were first outta the water."

We all became thoughtfully silent. Finally Joe spoke. "Bull, you have finally lost your little mind. We need to put you in the crazy house and locked away for good. It's a miracle we're all alive and not mortally wounded or dead."

I pondered Bull's determination. "Bull's right. We could at least talk about another plan."

Finally Joe agreed to listen. The new plan appeared to be not as dangerous as the first.

Mr. and Mrs. Berrynhill were goin' over to Romeo the comin' Saturday mornin' and spend the night with Mrs. Berryhill's father and mother, the Markham family. Bull wanted to take the old Model A truck, which had been converted from a regular Model A car. A small wooden bed was bolted to the back of the trunk and the cab was closed in by boltin' boards to the edge of metal. It wasn't a pretty sight, but it ran good. The Berryhill's planned to ride over to the Markhams with Mr. Berryhill's sister and her husband. The Model A would be available.

Bull explained, "All we need to do is get a noose 'round that 'gator again and then ease out and tie a rope to the end of the cable. We can rev up that old Model A and drag that damn gator outta that bar pit. Once he's out, he'll roll hisself up in that cable and at the same time, we'll rope him. We'll have that big rascal."

Joe almost died laughin', "Bull, what if that 'gator drags that old Model A into the bar pit? Do you know what Pa will do to all of us includin' Jack? Worse yet, think about Ma and then there's Jack's parents."

"Ain't no way that 'gator can drag that Model A into the borrow pit," said Bull.

We all thought over the situation, and I finally said, "We need to go back to the bar pit and see if we can find what's left of the catchpole. We can't do nothin' without that catchpole."

The next evenin', we went back over to the borrow pit and found the cable and catchpole close to the edge of the bank. Without pressure on the cable, it was easy for the 'gator to get loose. We looked around the borrow pit but didn't see the 'gator. Somehow, we all felt he was close around. The next evenin' we patched up the catchpole and were ready for a big Saturday night.

The Berryhill family left early on Saturday mornin'. That left us with plenty of plannin' time and time to finish cuttin' a cord of wood. About dark, we headed for the borrow pit. We drove down the road to the cut-off to the borrow pit. The cut-off was a dirt road that was almost covered with small wax myrtle. Bull turned off the lights, and we turned around and backed up close to the bank of the borrow pit where we last encountered the 'gator.

"Okay," said Bull, "Tie that rope to the bumper of the truck and to the end of the cable."

Joe and I got everythin' set to pull out that 'gator. We eased up to the edge of the bank, which was about three feet above the edge of the water. Bull reached up and turned on his headlight. Like magic, there was the 'gator, not twenty feet from the edge of the bank. It was as if he were expectin' us.

"Wonder how long he's been waitin' for us?" I curiously asked.

"He's likely been plannin' on us for his supper," replied Joe, "and since Bull is biggest and ugliest, he'll likely et him first."

"Get serious," said Bull calmly. "Let me see if I can call him a little closer."

Bull made his baby 'gator sounds, and we waited. Finally, we checked on the 'gator and he had moved closer. Maybe only twelve feet away but he had not sunk.

"I don't like the idea of tryin' to put a noose around his head if he don't sink," said Joe.

"Let me throw a small rock close to him and see if he'll sink," I said.

"Okay," replied Bull.

I threw a small rock about five feet from the 'gator, and he sunk. We eased out, dropped the noose close to his head and slowly slipped it under his head. We hardly disturbed him. We eased back as far as we could while Bull got ready to crank the Model A. The motor slowly turned over and died. The battery was dead.

"Quick, get the hand crank, Bull," said Joe.

Bull found it, and rushed to the front of the Model A. With blessed luck, it cranked on the first try. Bull rushed back inside the Model A, revved it up, and tightened the noose on the 'gator. The most unbelievable fight between the Model A and 'gator was burned forever into our memories. The 'gator was winnin'. The Model A could not get good traction on the grassy bank. The truck was slowly slidin' backward toward the edge of the bank. The throttle was wide open. No doubt this battle could be heard half way across the hammock. It's a wonder we didn't draw a crowd that included the game warden!

Bull hollered at me to cut the rope. Both Joe and I fumbled for our frog-skinnin' knives. We started slashin' at the rope. The Model A slipped within a foot of the edge of the bank before. A successful cut finally released the gator. The 'gator made a final giant slosh with his huge tail. He was gone.

We were left in total, dumb silence. Bull had shut off the Model A.

Finally Bull said, "Joe, it's okay for you to make a Jesus statement if it's a thankful one."

I'm not thinkin' about no Jesus statements," Joe replied. "I'm thinkin' that we won't live through another easy money plan this summer. We must swear to never tell a livin' soul. The entire town and county will be laughin' about three idiot boys, a giant 'gator, and a nearly lost Model A!"

Those Were the Times

Stories by Jack Foley

Chapter 3

The Surprise at Sand Slough

More than a week passed before Joe, Bull, and I began to talk amongst ourselves and laugh about the gator catchin' episode. This was forever to be one of our well-kept secrets. The only other person who knew 'bout this was Nathan Curney, and he gave his word he'd not tell.

On Sunday afternoon, we decided to go into Gulf Hammock, visit my parents, and stop by and visit Nathan Curney. He was usually on his front porch every Sunday afternoon. We left around noon, and walked out the small dirt road that went by the Berryhill place to the edge of Highway 19/98. We followed 19/98 north by Gavin's Store, which was closed on Sunday, and on to Peek's Store. It was open. We bought Pepsi's and an extra one for Nathan. He was on the front porch.

"Lord almighty, if it ain't dem gator catchin' rich folk. I thought ya'll would be drivin' a fancy automobile by now," greeted Nathan with a smile.

"You oughta not poke fun Nathan 'cause somethin' bad may happin' to you one day," I replied. "Besides, we bought you a Pepsi."

"My! My! No more pokin' fun at folk that buys a po man a Pepsi. What's ya'll up to now?" asked Nathan.

"Not much." Joe replied. "We're gonna visit Jack's Ma and Pa and mosey back toward home."

"Bull," Nathan asked, "ain't you spoze to look out for these other two? Why ain't they in church?"

"They likely should be, Nathan. Both of them could stand a little church goin'," replied Bull.

"Nathan, do you think if we had went to church more, that Jesus would have helped us catch that gator?" asked Joe.

"Jesus likely kept that gator from catchin' you," replied Nathan. "By the way, speakin' of catchin', I was down at the big curve on the way to Lebanon Station where Sand Slough crosses 19/98. I noticed a lot of fish trapped in a small spot where the water's dryin' up. I bet you could sneak in there with a seine and drag out a lot of fish. It's just a short way down Sand Slough where there are pockets of water. I could sell a lot of bass and good size bream over in the quarters."

"That's against the law," I replied. "Both the seinin' in fresh water and sellin' fresh water fish," I reminded him.

"It sure the hell is if you get caught," said Nathan. "They'd put colored folks under the jail but wouldn't do nothin' to three nice white boys."

"You're mostly Indian and only part colored so maybe they wouldn't do nothin' to you," I pointed out.

"The law don't think part colored, and besides, part Indian ain't too smiled on either," said Nathan.

"How much money do you think we could make?" asked Joe.

"Don't hardly know," replied Nathan. "It depends on how many fish you get."

"We'd better think this over," said Bull quickly. We need to put more distance between us and that gator catchin' mess."

We walked on to my house and visited with Ma and Dad. Both were concerned about Jack's brother, Fred, goin' to war. I'll tell you one thing for sure, if the Germans were lookin' for a fight, he is the right person. We talked some about Fred and other Gulf Hammock boys that had gone to war.

As we left Gulf Hammock on our way back to the Berryhill place, we began to make a plan to seine the area at Sand Slough.

"Are we really goin' to seine that pocket of water?" asked Joe.

"First off," replied Bull, "we don't have a seine and second, we don't have no way to carry the fish to Nathan." We are mighty lucky to even be walkin' around after that gator incident. Joe paid no attention to Bull's warnin'.

"When will Ma and Pa go back to visit with Grandpa and Grandma Markham?" wondered Joe aloud. "We need that A Model."

"They're goin' next Saturday," answered Bull. "It's Grandma Markham's birthday, and I know they'll stay over 'till Sunday. Probably they'll go with Uncle Woodrow like they did last time. The Model A would be available." We knew we had better do a lot of serious thinkin' before jumpin' into this, but knew Bull had already bought in.

"I been thinkin'," I said. "Why wouldn't chicken wire make a good seine? The mesh holes are little, and we could put small posts on each end of a piece of chicken wire and with one of us in the middle, we could pull every fish outta a small area. Nathan said it was a small area.

"Where we gonna get chicken wire?" asked Joe.

"Well," said Bull, "we got chicken wire around the chicken house...enough to make a seine. But remember, don't you two say I didn't warn you."

Joe exploded. "You are outta your mind. Totally outta your mind. Where's the chickens gonna be while we pull out the staples in posts holdin' the chicken wire and what 'bout gettin' it back up before Ma and Pa gets back? We lucked out by not gittin' killed by that damn gator, but this is for certain leadin' to big trouble."

"Let's at least think this over," I replied. "Why can't we wait 'til the chickens go to roost in the chicken house, lock the chickens up, and then take down the chicken wire?

We could put it back up before the chickens get up on Sunday mornin'. What do you think?"

Bull thoughtfully replied, "It may work. We'll plan some more this week before we decide, and we have to figure how to get the fish to Nathan. We'd need ice unless we took them late Saturday night. He'd have to know ahead for him to have some ice."

It was almost dark when we came up to the front gate of the Berryhill's. That week, as we cut and split our cords of wood, we carefully went over our plans. Mrs. Berryhill needed a few things from Gavin's Store and sent us to pick them up. We ran on to Nathan's house, caught him at home and let him know of our possible plan...if it all worked out.

By noon on Friday, we had the cord of wood and asked Joe and Bull's parents about tryin' to catch a few fish at the borrow pit. We ran most of the way to Sand Slough—about three miles—to check out the seinin' area. We made good time and easily found where Nathan told us where the fish were trapped. The water was dark, but you could see a lot of swirlin' movement in the water. There was a heavy grassy area around the edges of the trapped water which made a perfect place to drag out our fish. We decided that we could drive the Model A down the bank of Sand Slough and up close to the trapped water. We could pull the seine from the opposite side toward the Model A and then use the lights and our headlights to gather up the fish. The plan was perfect!

On Saturday mornin', Mrs. Berryhill's last words were a stern warnin' for us to stay out of trouble before she and Mr. Berryhill left for Romeo.

Early that afternoon, we became anxious to get on with our plan but no way were the chickens ready to go to roost that early.

"Any way we can git these damn chickens to git in that chicken house a little early?" asked Joe. "I'm ready to git that chicken wire down and git it ready to go."

"Won't be easy," responded Bull. "These chickens are scattered all over."

"Why can't we git some chicken feed and at least try to get them inside the chicken pen. Then we could chase them into the chicken house," I suggested.

"We could try," responded Bull, "but don't use much feed or Ma will notice that more than usual is gone."

Only about half of the chickens cooperated. We shut them in the pen and chased them all around but didn't manage to get all of them in the chicken house. Some flew over the fence, and when you'd open the chicken house door to run some in, others would run out. We ended up runnin' every single chicken until it became exhausted and carried each one to the chicken house. It was one big mess tryin' to get these chickens into the chicken house that early. Finally, after more than an hour of chicken chasin', we had them all in the chicken house.

"Bull, did you notice that some of those chickens were so tired they lay sideways on the ground and couldn't get up on the roost?" asked Joe. "What if they all die from heart attacks or heat strokes?"

Bull replied, "I don't think you could ever make up a lie good enough that Ma or Pa would believe about how all them chickens died. Maybe we'd better tell the truth if it happens."

"If half them chickens are dead in the mornin', I'm headin' for home," I replied.

"You just better pray them chickens are okay," said Bull. "Better yet, I better pray 'cause I know I could throw a rock higher than you or Joe's prayers would go."

We decided it was best to wait and see, but for now we needed to get the chicken wire down, make our seine, and head for Sand Slough.

The chicken wire was six feet tall with a one inch mesh. One section of the chicken wire was around thirty-five feet long. That was long enough for our seine, so we left the rest of the pen up. We got two older posts to attach to each end and one to roll up the inside of the chicken wire. We rolled up our seine and loaded it on the back of the Model A and headed on to Sand Slough. We took three fishin' poles in case someone saw us. We would pretend to be cat fishin'. We got to Sand Slough just at dark, drove along the bank, and backed the Model A into the edge of the woods where it wouldn't be seen from the highway. We worked in the dark gettin' the seine ready since our frog giggin' headlights could attract attention. We knew game wardens came along ever so often or maybe just some curious folks could happen to see us. We were ready! The Model A was pulled up to provide us light to get our fish, but we would not turn the lights on until we had pulled the seine across the trapped area of water.

"Bull, why don't you get the middle of the seine," said Joe. "Jack and I will get each end. We'll move slow, keepin' the fish in front of the seine then at the very end, we'll drag them up on the edge of the bank in front of the Model A. I'll turn on the Model A lights, and we can also use our headlights to throw the fish into the crocker sacks." Each of us had a large crocker sack ready.

"Lordy, it's black dark," said Joe.

"Guess it's a new moon," replied Bull, "But we'd better not use our headlights now."

They started slowly across the trapped water with Bull holdin' the middle of the seine on the bottom to keep fish from escapin' under the seine. 'Bout half way across, Joe exclaimed, "My God, we've got bushels of fish in front of this seine. It's gettin' hard to pull."

"It's really hard to keep this middle down," said Bull "and I'm boggin' down bad here in the middle. Let's try to move faster. The slower we go the deeper I'm sinkin' in this mud."

We put all our combined strength into movin' the seine faster. Fish were jumpin' over and goin' under the seine at the end. With our last effort, we dragged ev'rythin' in the seine out of the water and up in front of the Model A.

"Quick, Joe," said Bull "turn on the Model A lights."

Joe ran to the edge of the Model A, turned on the lights, and quickly followed me and Bull as he turned on his headlight. I turned on my headlight 'bout the time the Model A lights came on. 'Bout the same time, Bull turned on his headlight.

"God Almighty!" hollered Bull. "Get into the Model A!"

He was in the Model A in about two large jumps. Both Joe and I were stunned for a moment. I had never seen so many snakes in one place in all my life. They were all mixed in with the fish! There were all kinds of water snakes includin' a number of cottonmouth moccasins. There were also turtles of all sorts along with three or four small gators. Snakes were movin' everywhere along with turtles, small gators, and flounderin' fish.

"Jesus!" hollered Joe, jumpin' back into the Model A.

In two bounds, we were both in the Model A with Bull. Snakes, fish, turtles, and the small gators were makin' their way back into the water. Dumbfounded, we watched our wigglin' fortunes get away.

After most of the snakes had made their way back into the water, Bull eased out of the Model A, rope in hand, and tied one end to the seine and the other to the Model A bumper. Bull pulled it away from the water area, rolled it up, and headed for home. None of us had anythin' to say on the way home nor while we put the chicken pen back up. We washed up at the pump by throwin' buckets of water at each other and then sat down on the edge of the porch.

"Anybody get snake bit?" asked Bull.

"I'm still too scared to look close," I replied. "Bull, have you or Joe ever in your life seen that many snakes in one place?" I asked.

"Hell no!" replied Bull. "Nor have I seen so many fish in one pile. We sure lost a ton of fish."

"Forget the fish," said Joe. "We are some lucky to get out of this mess without bein' snake bit all over our bodies, and I got more to say. 'Member that plan we had to catch that big gator? Ya'll didn't learn squat from that and it was all our own doin'. Now Nathan Curney talked us up to puttin' another cockeyed plan together that came even closer to gettin' us all killed or mortally hurt. I've still got chills all over from thinkin' 'bout jumpin' through them snakes to get to the Model A. I tell you it would be a total cure for constipation if you didn't have a heart attack first. I ain't never gonna be no part of any plan that either of you come up with again."

"Joe," I said, "you were just as big a part of the plan as me or Bull and besides, I think we learned somethin' from this whole mess."

"Just what the hell did we learn?" asked Joe.

"Well, said Bull thoughtfully, "I learned not to try 'n put them damn chickens to roost early again and not to listen to anymore plans from you or Jack. I'll also alert Ma to any new plans suggested by you or Jack!"

"Will you also tell her that you were a big part of our plans?" asked Joe.

Stories by Jack Foley

Those Were the Times

Chapter 4
Wild Hogs and Catch Dogs

A few days after the seinin' disaster, Joe, Bull, and I were sittin' on the back porch of the Berryhill house and noticed Mr. Berryhill walkin' along the chicken pen lookin' carefully at the section we had used as a seine. He also looked at the staples we had nailed back into the posts. He glanced at us as he walked over to the edge of the porch.

"Boys," he said, "have you noticed that some of the meshes in that chicken wire seems to have been growin' pond grass? It's mostly dead now but hadn't been dead long. Ain't that strange?"

Joe, as usual, responded quickly. "Well Pa, I think it got there when we were throwin' water on each other usin' the same old buckets we used to bring home the fish we caught at the borrow pit. The buckets pro'bly still had some grass left in them."

"Son," Mr. Berryhill replied, "you have a gift for good stories, but I have a notion there's more to that one. All of you just be careful."

I began to breathe much easier as I was a little afraid of Mr. Berryhill. He was a large, fierce lookin' man with piercin' black eyes that seemed to see through any protective shield you put up...either with words or looks. He was covered with black hair, had a dark beard, and a small bald spot at the very top of his head. I later learned that Mr. Berryhill was a very kind and gentle person.

"I think it's about time you boys began to train Suzie's puppies to hunt hogs. We could use some fresh pork," said Mr. Berryhill.

"How 'bout us not havin' to cut a cord of wood this week and hog hunt instead. Couldn't we bring home a good sized sholt 'stead of cuttin' wood?" asked Joe.

"How 'bout two good sized sholts?" asked Mr. Berryhill.

The deal was done, and we began to plan to do some hog huntin'.

Susie was what they called a brindle dog which has to do with color rather than breed. She was one fine catch dog. Suzie was quick, smart, and extra strong. She would trail and chase a wild hog 'til the hog was bayed. To bay was when the wild hog stopped and decided to fight rather than run anymore. A hog usually bayed in an oak or palmetto scrub or in some area where the dog had to face the hog head-on with the hog's rear protected by the thick undergrowth or a good size tree.

Now there ain't nothin' any meaner or more dangerous than a wild boar hog with two long sharp tusks protrudin' up from his lower bottom jaw. He flat knows how to use these tusks and can rip open and kill a dog or mortally wound a person. Suzie would bay a wild hog but would never make an attempt to catch the hog until someone came to help, and then she still would wait for a signal to go ahead. If the hog charged Suzie before anyone came to help, she would outrun the hog but continue her efforts to bring the hog back to bay. It was critical for someone to assist the dog when the effort was made to catch the hog or the catch dog ended up injured or killed. No gun was allowed in the Berryhill hog claim area as it was a federal wildlife preserve, so catch dogs and trap pens were the only legal means of catchin' hogs.

They had caught a number of hogs with Susie before she had had four puppies which were now almost four months old. The puppies' father was a Redbone hound named Preacher Man. This old hound spent most of his time huntin' fine lookin' females that were kind' a hopin' a male like old Preacher Man would drop by. Preacher Man belonged to a colored family named Jenings who lived about a mile away, but Preacher Man spent most of his time wanderin' and lookin'. Ain't no tellin' how many dogs in the area were part Redbone hound. Bull, Joe and I agreed that Preacher Man had a great idea. It would be excitin' to have nothin' to do but go around the hammock lookin' for pretty girls. Only thing is that pretty girls' kin are really protective. We could get in more trouble than tryin' to catch another large gator.

Susie's puppies, like most young dogs, were lookin' for action. We had carried them on a couple of hog hunts, but kept them on leashes. They had watched as Suzie had caught a hog on two different trips, and it was hard to hold them back to keep them from chargin' the hog. That could surely get them hurt badly or killed. It ain't easy to train young dogs, but we did need some more hog dogs.

Now there is only one catch dog in a group of trained dogs. All dogs join in the trailin', chasin' and bayin' of a hog but make no effort to catch the hog. They keep the hog at bay by standin' a short distance from the hog and continuin' their barkin' until someone joins to help. If the hog charges, all the dogs scatter and try to bring the hog back to bay. Only the catch dog, with someone helpin', will move in for the catch with the other dogs watchin' and barkin'.

There ain't nothin' more excitin' than watchin' a catch dog move in on a wild hog when its given the go-ahead and you are movin' in with the dog to help with the catch. The catch dog will slowly move toward the hog with the hog makin' snappin' sounds with its teeth. The hog will charge the dog when the dog gets too close. The dog will quickly make a move that places it along side of the chargin' hog and at the same time, the dog will sink its teeth into the top of the hog's ear next to the hog's head. The hog will try all kinds of moves tryin' to shake the dog away from their side where they can use their tusks and teeth. As both the hog and dog turn, you have to catch the hog by the bottom of the hind legs, raise up the rear of the hog by the hind legs, turn the hog over on its side, and put one of your feet on the side of its head. Leather strips, like boot laces, are then used to tie the back legs of the hog together. Then the front legs are tied the same way. Finally the front and the back legs are tied together. It's also a good idea to tie the hog's snout closed. When you have the hog under control, the catch dog will release the hog's ear. If you don't help the catch dog quickly, the hog will turn and shake furiously and will get the catch dog in front. Then the catch dog will be badly hurt or killed, especially if the hog is a boar with good sized tusks. If the hog is a fairly young sholt, there is not much danger, but the dog and the person helpin' on the catch can still get hurt. Even a sholt can do some damage. The main role of all the dogs, except the catch dog, is to keep a hog at bay.

Mr. Berryhill operated a piece of heavy equipment that was used to skid logs out to a tram road where a loader would load them on flat cars and a train would pull the flat cars to the lumber mill. He got up at 4:30 a.m. every work day. He called us just before leavin' for work at the beginnin' of our hog huntin' week. When we didn't get up right away, Mrs. Berryhill called us. "Okay you boys, you made a deal, so you'd better get yourselves goin'. Breakfast is ready."

When Mrs. Berryhill called, no one dared sleep any longer.

"We'll be there in just a minute," called Bull.

We ate breakfast and began our plans.

"Let's go through by Boggy Pond, and if we don't jump a hog there, we can go on in that large open area by the borrow pit," suggested Joe. "We've seen all kinds of hog signs in that area."

"Jack, why don't you get those short pieces of rope we've used for leashes for those puppies?" said Bull. "It's gonna be a pain tryin' to teach them young idiots anythin'."

"Think them young dogs are ready for this?" I asked.

Both Bull and Joe replied, "No!" at the same time.

Joe added, "We done made a deal with Pa to try and train 'um and not one of 'em have the sense of a goose."

"Maybe we can jump a hog that'll feel sorry for 'em and help with the trainin'," I responded. "Anyway, it's gotta be easier than what Mrs. Chancey went through in the third grade tryin' to teach them Crowley boys how to read."

"Them little dummies never did learn to read very good," said Joe with a laugh, "but they beat Jack's butt every time they caught him alone."

"It took 'em both," I responded quickly.

"Look," said Bull, "if Mrs. Chancey had tusks and was as mean as one of those wild hogs, she could have had them Crowley boys readin' in no time. All she had to do is say 'read or else'. They weren't stupid. They were just lazy, and their parents likely couldn't read."

"Forget the Crowley boys," I replied, "I'd rather think about this hog hunt."

We leashed the young dogs and started through a dirt trail to Boggy Pond. It was most impossible to calm down the four young dogs as they were jumpin', barkin', and strainin' at the leashes. Suzie would look back at these puppies ever so often as if she were ashamed of all four of them.

As we got closer to Boggy Pond, the growth became thicker. The pond was surrounded by some giant cypress trees. There were areas of thick oak scrubs and palmetto thickets close to the edges of the pond. We looked for fresh hog signs, but didn't find any fresh enough for Suzie to trail. Suzie carefully sniffed different areas but found no hot trail spots. We decided to move on through to the large open area that surrounded the borrow pit. The workers that built up the Highway 19 roadbed before 1940 had dug this borrow pit and used the dirt for fill. The borrow pit covered six or so acres, and the openin' was maybe twenty or so acres. As we came out into the edge of the openin' Suzie stopped. Her eyes were fixed on the far corner of the cleared area. We all looked in that direction. As usual, Suzie was right. There were three wild hogs busy rootin' in search of food and they hadn't noticed us yet.

"Wait, Suzie," said Bull as he knelt beside her with his arm around her neck. "Do you think we should turn these puppies loose to help Suzie bay one of these hogs?"

"No," said Joe. "They'll try to catch the hogs instead of bayin' them. We'd better let Suzie get one at bay and try to show the puppies how to stay at a distance and just hold the hog at bay."

"I like that idea best." I responded.

"Okay," Bull replied, "ya'll hold these puppies." Bull hollered, "Go get 'em Suzie," and she was off like a shot.

Suzie didn't look back until the hogs saw her comin', and she was mighty close to them by then. They ran off with Suzie on their heels. She bayed one, really quick, in a thick oak and palmetto scrub. There was a narrow trail into the scrub. The hog had used the trail to go into the scrub, then turned around and was facin' Suzie when they got to the edge of the scrub. You could hear the wild hog poppin' his teeth. Suzie's barkin' told you the hog was at bay.

The puppies were goin' wild. They were jumpin', barkin', and strainin' at the leashes. I was tryin' to hold all four of the puppies, and they were hard to hold.

"Do ya'll think it's a good idea to turn them loose?" I asked.

"Joe, let's me and you get a piece of one of these scrubs and try to teach the puppies to mind and not to try to attack that hog," said Bull. "Switch their asses if they try to go for the hog. Maybe they'll keep a distance."

I continued to hold the four puppies while Bull and Joe cut a piece of the scrub oaks that would make a stout switch to use on any dog that tried to catch the hog.

"Turn 'em loose now," said Bull.

I quickly untied the puppies. It's real hard to believe what all happened in the next few minutes. All four puppies got around Joe and Bull, but not before they attacked the hog and got their asses beat. Suzie looked on, at a distance, with disgust. I really believe she was totally ashamed of her off-spring. I guess that's true of mothers all over the world that has idiot off-spring. Especially if they ain't even trainable.

I was on the outer edge of the scrub when the puppies attacked the hog. The hog used its strong snout and shoulder to toss the first puppy high into the air and over the top of the scrub. They do this by bringin' their snout up under the belly of the dog and slingin' it up into the air. If the hog had tusks, the dog would have been ripped open but this young male hog had only very small tusks which caused only a little damage to the puppy.

It was hard for me to believe my eyes as I saw the first puppy in the air, just over the top of the scrub. The puppy was still runnin'. His legs were churnin' in the air while he continued both barkin' and howlin'. Down he went and then right back into the scrub but not before there were two more puppies in the air. It looked like someone was jugglin' puppies over the top of a scrub. By now, both Bull and Joe had seen the jugglin' act and were tryin' to catch and tie up the puppies. I watched for a minute more and then pitched in to catch and tie up puppies. Suzie continued to try and keep the hog at bay. Finally, the puppies were leashed and tied to a small oak scrub.

"Okay, Jack," said Bull, "it's about your turn to catch a wild hog. You haven't caught one before, and it's not the same as watchin' me or Joe catch one. Remember, a hog that size can do you some damage with his teeth. Give Suzie the go-ahead and move in with her."

I had watched Bull and Joe catch hogs before but had not given it a try. I moved cautiously in back of Suzie and said "Okay Suzie, let's catch that hog." Suzie began to move slowly toward the hog backin' up as Suzie moved closer. I kept back around eight feet. In case the hog got by Suzie, I would have a chance to jump off the trail and into the scrub. That would give the hog a chance to get by without chargin' me. I could feel my heart beatin' a little harder and some fear creepin' in. I thought, *it's too late to think of fear, goose bumps, rapid heartbeat, or anythin' else 'cept to catch that hog.*

Suzie kept movin' closer and the hog began to increase the poppin' sound he made with his teeth. He began to get more wild eyed. Finally, Suzie was close to four feet from the hog. He charged. Suzie made her quick turn and was along side the hog, sinkin' her teeth at the top of the hog's ear. She dug her feet in and forced the hog to make a turn. On the second turn the hog made, he had his rear to me. I jumped in. I grabbed both hind legs just above the ankles. I lifted the hog's rear up in the air. I will forever remember what happened next. That hog shook me so hard with those rear legs that I thought my elbows and shoulder joints were wrecked for life. I felt my eyeballs shakin' in my sockets. I simply could do nothin' but hold onto the hog as he continued the shakin'.

I could hear both Bull and Joe holler. "Throw that hog over on his side! Throw that hog over on his side!"

Suzie hung on with her body pressed against the body of the hog, and I got the shakin' of my life. Some way or another I crossed the hog's back legs and turned him over on his side and got my foot on his neck. Bull and Joe rushed in and tied the hog's back and front legs and then tied his snout shut. Susie turned the hog loose as soon as he was goin' over on his side and then moved a short distance from the hog. She watched closely while the hog was tied. She didn't even look over at the loud mouth puppies that were still barkin' and bouncin' around tryin' to get back to the hog. I went out past the edge of the scrub and sat down under a small scrub oak. I thought for sure I had some type of permanent damage, possibly brain damage. Bull and Joe tied the hog to a small scrub oak where he couldn't move around and came over to where I was searchin' for injuries.

Bull said with tears in his eyes from laughin', "Jack, you done a damn good job shakin' that hog. He'll likely never be the same."

"You must have been havin' fun since you shook him awhile before throwin' him over on his side. Suzie was wonderin' what the hell was goin' on," added Joe with a big smile.

"Ain't no time for funnin'," I replied. "I still can't focus my eyes. I just couldn't see to jerk that hog's rear up and turn him on his side in one motion and I, for sure, ain't lookin' for more practice today."

"Well," said Bull, "we need one more hog today, and we have made our side of the deal with Pa."

"No way," said Joe, "we got all week to get two sholts, and if we get two today, we'll be back cuttin' wood by tomorrow."

"Mr. Berryhill said we could hunt hogs all week." I replied. "It wouldn't matter none if we caught two hogs now, just as long as we got two."

"Then let's just try 'n get our two now since we know there's two more around here, and they won't be far away," said Bull. We all agreed and put the puppies on leashes and set Suzie to trailin' the two hogs that got away. The trail was fresh, and Suzie had no problem in bayin' one of the two that got away not far from where we caught the first one. It was difficult to hold the puppies on leashes as they were goin' wild for more action. No way were we goin' to let them loose again.

"I'll catch this one," said Bull. He gave Suzie the go-ahead, and we moved in on the young hog. Bull was experienced at this, and he and Suzie made the catch look easy. I will forever know it's not as easy as Bull made it look. We tied up the hog, cut a small pine saplin' and made it into a carryin' pole, stuck it between the hog's back and front legs, and with one of us on each end, and the hog upside down in the middle, we carried the hog out to where the first hog was staked out. We headed on back to the Berryhill's, and Mr. Berryhill decided to go back with us. We noticed some large bream and a couple of bass were beddin' close to the bank of the borrow pit while we were loadin' the hogs. We decided to fish the next day instead of hog huntin'.

The fishin' was really good that Tuesday mornin'. We caught a good string of large bream and five good size bass. We got back home in early afternoon, and Mrs. Berryhill was pleased with the fish and planned a fish fry for that evenin'. She gave us fifteen cents to go to Gavin's Store for each of us to get a Pepsi. When we got back, we cleaned fish and put screw worm medicine on minor scrapes the puppies got from their hog fight. This would keep the blow flies away and keep them from gettin' screw worms.

The group then headed for Gavin's Store and began to make plans for doin' some more hog huntin' on Wednesday. We never suspected a terrible tragedy would happen on that day.

We left early Wednesday mornin' with Suzie in the lead and with the puppies left in a pen at home. You could hear them barkin' and howlin' 'til we got out of sight. They really wanted to go, but we had decided against any more trouble that week. While we were fishin' at the borrow pit on Monday, we had come back home through the woods by Boggy Pond and saw some fresh hog signs on the edge of one side of Boggy Pond. We headed straight for that area. As we neared the hog signs, Susie gave signs of excitement. She circled the area and picked up a fresh scent. She barked a couple of times and began to trail deeper into the woods. Suzie would only bark once in a while to let you know where she was when she trailed, but she would bark loud and steady when she began the chase and continued the barkin' when she bayed.

We heard when Suzie caught sight of the hog and began the chase. We ran as fast as we could through some thick wooded areas. We were close when she bayed and then heard her holler in pain. We saw a large boar charge out of the area where Suzie had been keepin' the boar at bay. The wild boar looked like he weighed over three hundred pounds with huge tusks protrudin' from his lower jaw. He came directly toward us. We scattered, and I got behind a cabbage palm. The boar saw us as he got within fifteen feet, and then he turned and headed deeper into the woods. We ran into the area where we had last heard Suzie. She was lyin' along the edge of a dirt trail that led into a thick oak scrub. The wild boar had charged her and somehow, she was not able to outrun him or get out of his path.

"God Almighty!" said Bull as he knelt beside Suzie. "She's cut from her shoulder across her belly to the edge of her back leg and her intestines are comin' out."

Susie was still alive but didn't make a sound. She had a mournful look in her eyes and foam runnin' out the edges of her mouth.

"What the hell are we goin' to do?" asked Joe thoughtfully. "Maybe try to sew her up?"

I got some rolled up fishin' line and some good size hooks," I said quickly.

We always carried fishin' line rolled on a short stick and fishin' hooks. We would always stop on our travels, cut a pole, and fish.

Bull said, "Jack, you and Joe straighten out the biggest hook you have and we'll press her intestines back in and try to sew her up."

Joe and I pressed her intestines back inside, and Bull began to sew her up. Suzie barely made a sound, and it took us awhile to complete the sewin'. Joe and I cut two small saplings and made two carry poles. We took off our shirts and threaded the poles through the sleeves and used fishin' line to tie down ends of the shirts and make a stretcher. We took turns, two at a time, and carried Suzie home. She was still alive when we got there. Mr. and Mrs. Berryhill could not believe she was still alive. Mrs. Berryhill poured liniment on the wound, and we built a cover over her to keep her out of the weather and placed her on blankets under a small shed. Two or three times a day, we would bring out food and feed Suzie by hand and hold her head up to give her water. Every day, we got up early and went straight to see her, always expectin' to find her dead.

Suzie lived! Not only did Suzie live, but she lived to hog hunt again. We decided to try and train the four puppies to coon hunt, and they became the best coon hounds in all the hammock. Preacher Man surely had to be proud of those four coon hounds.

Not long after Suzie began to hunt again, I decided to go back and live at home. My parents were always glad to see me come back home. I was lucky to have two homes, the Berryhills and my parent's place.

The Author's Historic Note

To hunt hogs in Levy County, you needed a legal hog claim for the area you were hunting or permission from the owner of the claim.

To obtain a hog claim for a specific area, it must be obtained at the courthouse in Bronson. Wild hogs in Greater Gulf Hammock are rather plentiful and dangerous. Traps or dogs are most often used.

The Author's Comment:

A large wild boar hog is the meanest and toughest animal in Greater Gulf Hammock. Also, a claim owner can get rather mean if they catch someone hog huntin' on their claim without permission.

Stories by Jack Foley

Those Were the Times

Chapter 5

Jumper Totin' Skinners, Blank Saturdays, and Juke Joints

I had heard some talk about skinners, blank Saturdays, and Juke Joints, and was interested in knowin' more. However, it's hard to get anyone who knows much to talk. I was hopin' to learn lots more as I had a summer job in the lumber yard. I had many opportunities to talk with some of the regular Negro workers, and I felt many of them would know a lot.

Dad had cooked breakfast and left enough on the back of the woodstove for the rest of the family. Breakfast was always the same—biscuits, gravy, bacon, and a pot of coffee. Me and Dad ate breakfast together and headed through the woods on the boardwalk to the mill. Dad stopped off at the planer mill where he graded lumber. I went over to the lumber yard where I was thirty minutes early.

Before long, Joe Berryhill and two more of my friends from the ninth grade—Spike Durden and Bruce Bass—showed up. I was surprised and pleased as I was not aware they had been hired for the summer. While we were talkin', Franklin Schuler showed up. He had been hired full-time as a regular lumber stacker. We were jokin' around when Mr. Slay showed up—the foreman of the lumber yard. Mr. Slay was about six feet tall, heavy set, with thick gray hair and a reddish complexion. He wore dark denim work pants, a matchin' denim work shirt, and a pair of new brogan work shoes.

Mr. Slay greeted the group of boys, "Hey boys—are ya'll ready to go to work?"

"Yes, sir," we all replied.

"Listen carefully," said Mr. Slay. "Here are your instructions."

"Spike, you and Bruce will be workin' full-time as stick boys. I'll have J.D. get both of you started. He will keep a check on you both, and he'll be along in a minute."

"Joe, you'll work as a part-time stacker with Samuel and help the stick boys when you're not stackin'. Samuel will be here shortly."

"Jack, I want you to quickly learn to use some tally sheets that will show how much lumber each pair of lumber stackers either tear down or put up each day. I'll show you how to fill out a tally sheet for each pair of stackers. It's very important to work fast the first thing in the mornin' and at quitin' time. Listen carefully. Be sure not to let them stackers bullshit you into showin' on the tally sheets that they did more than they really did. Can I trust you with this job?"

"Yes sir!" I quickly replied.

Joe left with Samuel and Bruce left with J.D. I went with Mr. Slay and quickly learned to fill out tally sheets.

We all had a fifteen minute break around 9:30 a.m. and 2:30 p.m. Durin' the first break, we all bought a soft drink from Sam Huff who came around sellin' 'em.

Joe was the first to start razzin' me. I knew it was comin'.

"Jack," Joe said in a loud voice. "Have you been kissin' up to Mr. Slay? Is that how you got that kissey little job?

That just opened the door for Spike and Bruce to chime in with their nasty little comments on how I managed to get the job. Everyone was enjoyin' the razzin' I was gettin'.

I quickly responded, "Well," I began in a loud voice. "Look what my supposed to be good buddies are really like. Now let me set the record straight."

Stories by Jack Foley

"I know that Mr. Slay took one look at the rest of you and one look at me. He could shorely see that I was much more handsome and smarter than you three morons."

"Ooooooooh," said Franklin, laughin'. "I shorely can see he can out bullshit all of you. I'm headin' back to my job for now, but I'll be back just after work to see how ya'll are goin' to deal with this smart ass boy."

"Yeah, Franklin," I responded. "You better do lots of stackin' and build up those scrawny muscles. I may decide to take up boxin' again, and I'll git you first."

"Lordy, lordy," Franklin said while walkin' away laughin' and shakin' his head.

I liked my new job. I got to talk to all the stackers as well as all the tractor drivers who pulled buggies of lumber to and from all areas of the lumber mill. That included the dry kiln, planer mill, box cars, and saw mill. The lumber yard covered more than 300 acres.

About two times a week, Mr. Slay would go to the Commissary Store, where the lumber mill offices were located, to turn in payroll information and other types of information requested by office personnel. All lumber yard workers knew exactly when he left and had a way of knowin' when he was goin' to return.

"The race was on!"

The tractor drivers quickly lined up, two abreast between runways of lumber with either lumber filled or empty buggies.

One of the most reckless of all drivers was Dollar Bill. He would tie a big black towel around his neck that would drop down his back like a cape. Dollar Bill wore a pull down cotton cap that rolled up to set on top of his head. He could roll down the cap over his face. He had cut two holes where he could see and called himself "The Drivin' Debo." The race lasted about twenty minutes.

One time, when I was watchin' the race, Debo turned over a buggy of lumber resultin' in a mad scramble to upright the buggy and quickly get the lumber back loaded. It was close to the time for Mr. Slay to return. A group of workers jumped in to help upright and load the buggy. Possum Lee warned all of us not to tell anyone what happened. Everyone agreed not to mention one word.

Mr. Slay was right about some of the stackers tryin' to bullshit me about how much lumber they stacked. I kept the tally sheets as accurate as possible. The stackers never gave up. They continued to try to give me numbers that was more than they stacked.

Mr. Slay looked carefully over the tally sheets each day and seldom made even a slight change. He said my work gave him more time to supervise.

One afternoon after work, I noticed a new Negro man laughin' and talkin' with a small group of stackers. He sure looked different. He was slightly taller than any of the stackers and was dressed in pressed denim pants, a matchin' denim shirt, and carried a matchin' denim jumper. He was a dandy! I was impressed with his friendliness and sense of humor. This man had a quick smile, sparklin' white teeth, and gave his name as James.

"Any of you boys want to beat me out of a dime or maybe two?" asked James with a big smile.

"What's yo' game?" asked Possum Lee.

"Well now," said James. "We could play a little three coin game or greasy pig or maybe spot the marble," responded James as he reached inside his jumper pocket and took out three small, open top boxes and a bright red marble.

James smoothed off a small spot on the ground and carefully placed the three boxes. He made sure everyone could see that he placed the marble under one of the boxes.

Again, with a big smile, James said, "Gonna bet one of you lucky gamblin' men a dime if you can guess which box that purty red marble is under."

Possum Lee responded quickly, "I knows 'xactly which its under. Now gimme that dime." The crowd that had gathered roared with laughter.

Stories by Jack Foley

"Now wait," shouted James. "You gotta wait 'til I move 'em around and then guess. I'm gonna give this man first guess if he will bet a dime."

"What's your name?" James asked Possum Lee.

"Name's Possum Lee, and I'll figure out if I'm gonna bet after I see yo moves.

James said, "Watch them boxes Possum Lee as I move them around and rather slowly." He stopped and looked up at Possum Lee.

"Wanna bet that dime?" asked James, again with that white sparklin' smile.

All of us were sure which box the marble was under and wanted to bet. However, James insisted Possum Lee had first choice.

"I'm gonna bet," said Possum Lee as he reached down and put his finger on top of the box.

James lifted the box and shouted, "Lordy, lordy! Ole Possum Lee done beat me outta a dime!" The crowd roared with laughter .

There were two more quick winners and the gamblin' fever began to set in. It was the first time I had ever felt a strong desire to gamble.

James began to move the boxes much faster, askin' for bets, and at the same time entertainin' the crowd with humor.

I lost a quarter in my first gamblin' game. It was all the money I had, and I was certain I would win. So, I could forget that Pepsi on the way home. As I left, the size of the crowd had increased to about ten workers. I was still sure I could win if I had a little more money to play with. It was then, I remembered I had a little money at home.

On Saturday mornin', I stopped by to see if Nathan Curney was home. Nathan had just returned from workin' his trap line. He greeted me as he was walkin' up to the porch.

"Well, bless my soul! If it ain't my good buddy dat got rich pickin' up dem stackin' sticks. Why don't you go on to Peek's Store and bring us back two Pepsi's?" Nathan tossed me a dime, and I returned quickly with our drinks.

Those Were the Times

"Tell me," Nathan said. "How's the stick boy's job?"

"Well now," I stated. 'I ain't no stick boy. My job is to use tally sheets and to keep up with how much lumber each pair of stackers stack or tear down each day."

"Now ain't you somethin'?" Nathan said with a smile on his face.

"Nathan," I said changin' the subject. "I want to tell you about a gambler who was on the lumber yard just after work yesterday. I explained how excitin' and entertainin' the game was and that the gambler would be comin' back one afternoon the comin' week to play some new games.

I told Nathan that I had played once and lost a quarter when I was sure I would win. I shared that I had never been so excited and I looked forward to the next week.

Nathan took a big drink of his Pepsi. He looked at me for what seemed to him to be a long time. I began to get nervous and fidgety.

Finally, Nathan said, "Jack, you have just met your first 'Jumper Totin' Skinner' and there's not just one of these type folks. There are lots of them. They work migrant camps, turpentine stills, lumber mills, Juke Joints, and other locations where laborers gather. They are called skinners 'cause they play a lot of skin games. They are called skin games 'cause folks who play with them git skinned! They carry a jumper because they have lots of pockets that are located inside and outside. Every pocket has one or more skin game. Skinners dress in fancy denims so they look good and can hold their games. They are good entertainers and they got good reasons to git everybody laughin' and in a good mood."

Nathan went on, "Jack, you have to have winners and losers. The skinner has to leave with more money than he came with, and losers can get ugly and mean. This means that a skinner lives a dangerous life. At times, they may be mighty lucky to get away with their life."

"Nathan," I asked. "Have you ever heard of a skinner gettin' killed here in Gulf Hammock?"

"Jack, there are some things you don't talk about," Nathan quickly replied.

I knew by Nathan's quick response that he would not say another word about skinners. I was curious. I could ask the Deputy Sheriff about the skinner, but I recently got in a fight with his son, and his son is a sore loser.

Then I thought maybe Franklin would know, and I would ask him on Monday if I didn't see him before on the weekend.

I got the idea, while thinkin' 'bout Nathan's remarks to his questions, that there had been some bad trouble with a skinner bein' killed or maybe a couple of skinners were beat up but managed to leave Gulf Hammock alive.

I wondered 'bout this and how often skinners coming through Gulf Hammock managed to peacefully skin money, and peacefully leave.

There was quite a spell that both Nathan and I were quiet and sat drinkin' our Pepsi's.

Nathan was the first to break the silence by askin', "Jack, just what did you learn from your experience of gamblin' with a skinner?"

I thoughtfully answered, "Nathan, I still might bet a little bit, just to be involved in all the excitement and get that fever feelin'. I would plan just to lose a little."

"That would be smart if you can do just that. However, the only reason you lost a little this past time is that the quarter was all you had."

Nathan went on, "You will need to learn you can't win playin' another man's game no more than chasin' the chaser and not get caught. It's much better to learn from a lost quarter than at a much higher cost."

We finished our Pepsi's, and I headed for home. I was thinkin' 'bout Nathan's advice and also 'bout the skinners and the dangerous life they lived. I wondered if they did risk their life for the little money they won from the workers. I had learned that workers had very little money from pay day to pay day.

Those Were the Times

I remembered when my family arrived in Gulf Hammock that the pay for workers was $.10 per hour for a ten hour day or $1 per day. Out of this pay, they had to pay for their housin' and a doctor's fee. Also, the activities that took place at the Juke Joints took a good part of money from many of the Negro workers.

When pay day was on a Saturday, and at least one Negro was not killed that night at one of the Juke Joints, it was called a "Blank Saturday."

There were five Negro quarters that belonged to the mill. They were Painted House, the Seven House, Odessa, Waccassassa, and the Crate Mill.

Over time, there were Juke Joints at the Painted House, Odessa, and the Crate Mill quarters. They all belonged to the mill.

I learned the most about a Juke Joint from Sandy Moore who ran one of the Juke Joints for a long period of time. Sandy, at one time, also worked with my dad over at the Planer Mill. I worked one summer there and became friends with Sandy. I even asked him if I could visit one Saturday night. Sandy said absolutely no. No whites were allowed. I did go by and visit Sandy one Sunday when the buildin' was closed.

The Juke Joint had a gamblin' room, a dance area, an area for the ladies, a dinin' area, a bar, and indoor facilities. The buildin' facilities were a vast improvement from the regular housin' for Negroes.

Sandy Moore was killed at the Juke Joint. The case was investigated by the High Sheriff, G.T. Robbins, but never solved. There were about twelve people present in the gambler's room when Sandy was killed, but nobody saw nothin'.

It was believed that many illegal activities went on at the Juke Joint. However, there was a belief that there would be no way to keep Negro laborers without Juke Joints.

The skinners visited the Juke Joints on a regular basis, and they depended highly on their charm and skills to make a few dollars and safely git out of town.

I finally did get a chance to talk to Franklin about the skinners. Franklin was very careful not to provide any specific information about fights or killin' that may involve skinners. He ended his conversation with me by askin' with a big smile, "Why do you want to know 'bout all this? Do you plan on killin' that skinner for takin' yo quarter?"

With that kind of response from Franklin, I knew my chance of findin' much information about skinners was slim 'ta none. I decided to forget about skinners and get up early Saturday mornin' and spend some time fishin'.

There is a good fishin' place in one of the clear creeks that flows near the Negro Maby Baptist Church located close to the Crate Mill Quarters. I always have good luck there. I was surprised when I saw they were havin' some kind of special service as I walked past the church on my way to the fishin' place. As usual, I did well.

The group at the church was endin' their service so I decided to wait for them to leave as I needed to go back by the church to go home. Finally things grew quiet. Then I got a shock. Someone, in a rather loud voice, asked, "What are you doin' here?" I looked in back of me and saw a large Negro man. He was very tall, maybe 6 feet, 7 inches. "Been doin' some fishin'," I answered. "My name is Jack Foley."

"I know who you are," he answered. "You are Albert Foley's boy. My name is Felix, and I'll call you Jack. I've seen you fishin' here before. I noticed you were fixin' to leave. Why don't you walk with me by the church. We have some great left-overs."

They had some of the best pie I've ever eaten. I learned that Felix had worked some in the loggin' woods, recently as a stacker on the lumber yard and was goin' to work with Will Safford at the Saw Mill.

As I started to leave, I had another shock. I was passin' by a window and saw a man inside the church. It was none other than James, the Skinner!

Felix was aware that I saw James. He asked me to sit down at one of the outside tables and talk a few minutes. Here is what Felix told me: "I am aware you have been askin' about skinners and this is all I will tell you. First, there are skinners and there are skinners, and other than gamblin', there not only can be, but there is, some big differences in certain skinners. I'll use James as one example. He has done wonders for some people that were hit by hard times. The Lumber Company has a policy that if a worker gits killed on the job, they are covered by a one hundred dollar insurance policy and no other benefits. Now stop an' think. There are very few jobs for Negro women—especially ones with young children. They can no longer live in the Quarters unless they can find another person to live with. I could point out the hard times they face, but I think you could guess. I'll start with that example. With James, there are many more. James limits the amount of money he uses gamblin'. With this, he keeps only the small amount necessary to live. He ain't in church much. All the money he gives goes to them that need it most. What I'm sayin' to you is there is at least one skinner that I know of that has been of great help to many that were in great need. There may be more than one like James. I don't know that."

Felix went on to say "That's all I'll tell you except I'm a part-time preacher and a story-teller. I'll be seein' you at the Green Chain. I know you work some there with Will Safford."

I walked on home havin' learned all I needed to know about "Jumper Totin' Skinners!"

Chapter 6

The Runaways

It was a long bus ride home with a lot of hollerin' and paper throwin'. Mrs. Mozo stopped the bus a number of times and threatened to put out all boys. Finally, most of 'em agreed not to aggravate her anymore.

I got off at Gavin's Store where I had worked part-time durin' the ninth grade. I did not mind tellin' Mr. Gavin at all that I was quittin', but I did mind tellin' Mrs. Gavin. I liked her, and she was always nice to me.

I walked back home, and my mother was surprised to see me.

"I didn't expect you until around 9:30 tonight. Are you not workin' for Gavin's this evenin'?" asked my mom.

"No ma'am," I replied. "I'm goin' to take a few days off and do a little fishin' and relaxin'. I'll try to get a job at the mill. The mill has great work hours compared to Gavin's."

When Dad got home, I explained I had quit Gavin's and wanted a job at the mill and that I would like to start after I had a week off. My dad laughed.

"I didn't know you put in that much hard work at school. However, I'll ask around about a job for you. Also, I hear you and Mr. C.D. Tummond got to know each other. He could be helpful in findin' you a job."

I had got to know Mr. C.D. Tummond through the boxin' matches at Peeks Store and through his sister who was in grade school with me. I made sure that I would stop by and see him at his office at the Commissary Store on Saturday mornin'. The company offices were all located at the Commissary Store, and C.D. worked as paymaster as well as other duties assigned by the owners or general manager. C.D. had started out as a laborer for the mill and that gave him identity with the other laborers.

I got up early on Saturday mornin' and headed for the Commissary Store. I stopped by Mr. Tummond's office, and he seemed a little surprised to see me there.

"Jack," C.D. asked, "what brings you around on an early Saturday mornin'?"

I explained my interest in a summer job.

"I think we could get you on at the lumber yard," responded C.D. "Check with me durin' the early part of the week, and I'll let your dad know if I see him first. He may find you somethin' at the planer's mill."

"Thank you," I replied. "I'll be checkin' in with you."

"By the way, if you catch more fish than you want this comin' week, drop me off a mess and make sure they are cleaned," said C.D. with a grin.

"I'll do it," I replied. "Just after you or Dad says I have a job startin' next week. I'll also cook 'em for you if you like."

I left the Commissary Store and decided to check on Nathan Curney and get his ideas on some good fishin' spots. I had planned on a peaceful comin' week wanderin' 'round in the hammock, but fate would work against me. An event the next week would occur that would bring both fear and weigh heavy on my mind for most the summer and maybe forever.

When I arrived at Nathan's house, I was met by his wife who was always pleasant.

"Jack," she smiled. "Nathan is down by the small pond just off the short-cut to Aunt Liza's. If you'd like to wait, he'll be back soon. I know he'd like to see you. Could I get you somethin' to drink?"

"No, ma'am," I replied. "I'll wander down that way, and if I can't find him, I'll come back by."

I went back through the short-cut toward Aunt Liza's house and cut off a dim trail that led by the edge of the pond. The pond was next to a wet hammock area and close to one of the small Wekiva creeks. The growth was thick in this area and spots were boggy.

I came up close to the edge of the pond when someone spoke to me in a deep, gruff voice that came from behind me, and it wasn't Nathan. I turned and was a little shocked to see a large colored man who I'd never seen before. He wore a pair of ragged overalls, a long sleeve, dirty denim shirt, and a worn out pair of brogan shoes. He had a beard and wore an old felt hat. His eyes were dark and piercin' and seemed to look right through me. At first, he scared the hell out of me. We stood lookin' at each other for what seemed a long time. I decided to make a run for it and turned to run for the creek but there was another colored man right in front of me. He looked much like the first man only younger. I tried to talk, but my voice quivered and didn't even sound like me. My heart was bangin' against my chest.

"I'm lookin' for Mr. Nathan Curney," I said in a shaky voice. "His wife told me he'd be here."

The older colored man answered, "Are you a friend of Mr. Nathan?" he asked.

"Yes sir," I quickly replied. "We've been friends a long time."

I began to feel a little safer now that we were talkin'. About that time, Nathan seemed to appear out of nowhere. He could go through the hammock like a ghost.

"Jack," Nathan said with a smile. "I see you done met up with these fine fellows. This older fella's name is Abraham, and his boy is named Jacob. Seems they escaped from one of 'em turpentine stills up north of the Suwannee River. They bin hidin' durin' the day, walkin' at night, and have made it to here. I found 'em at the edge of the woods last night. They were close to my trap line. I got 'em some food and a couple of blankets. Now I don't know what to do with 'em. They got a deputy and a turpentine fellow after 'em

Those Were the Times

'cause they owe 'em money at the turpentine still Commissary Store and they got to work it off. Course, ain't never gonna happen at most turpentine stills. It's like slavery. They'll likely be beat if they ever catch 'em. They'll take 'em back to the turpentine still."

I listened with interest as Nathan explained the situation.

My initial reaction was to simply say it ain't my problem and move on toward the house. Deep down, I knew I couldn't do that. I'd heard about the terrible practices at some turpentine stills.

"Jack," Nathan said in a determined voice. "I got to try to help these people. Let's just all sit down on a dry log and talk and eat some vittles. I got a bag of stuff here."

I felt a sense of desperation and at the same time helplessness. Suddenly, I wasn't hungry and couldn't even drink one of the Pepsi's Nathan brought. Everybody ate in silence. Nathan noticed I wasn't eatin'.

"Jack," Nathan said quickly. "Drink your Pepsi and stop worryin' 'bout this situation. We'll figure somethin' out."

"Nathan," I replied. "There's just nothin' I know I can do to help, and this whole situation kinda' scares me."

Nathan laughed, "Now that's a surprise since I know you ain't exactly the scary type. We just need some plan to help these folks out."

"Nathan," I quickly responded. "You remember some of my big plans such as catchin' that big gator and then draggin' out all those snakes with that chicken wire seine? My plans darn near got me, Joe, and Bull bad hurt or maybe killed. I best listen to your plans."

Abraham spoke up, "Look, Mr. Nathan. 'Hits better we let dis white boy go if'n he don't tell nobody 'bout us. He could git in trouble wif de law."

"I think Jack can help us," responded Nathan. "I got a good idea that we could try. Jack is friends with Mr. C.D. Tummond who is the paymaster with the lumber mill. Maybe if Mr. C.D. would hire Abraham and Jacob and agree to pay off their Commissary Store debt at the turpentine still, I don't think no deputy or the turpentine people would git no fight with 'em mill owners. They too big and powerful for 'em turpentine people. Besides, 'em turpentine people usually lease rights to get turpentine off mill owner's lands."

"Nathan," I responded. "You thinkin' I should go and ask Mr. C.D. Tummond 'bout this idea?"

"It may work," said Nathan. "While we wait, we gotta keep Abraham and Jacob hid and make sure you don't tell Mr. C.D. where they are."

"Wait!" I said. "I ain't said I'd do anythin' yet. What if the constable finds out these two may be in around here. If he found I even had anythin' to do with this, he'd try and have my hide. I knows he's a crook and gits out on the highway and shakes down tourists and arrests poor laborers for stupid reasons just to get some pay for each arrest. You know that after that fight I had with his boy that he's been mad with me. If it wasn't for my older brother and Dad, he'd have hauled me off to the Bronson jail already."

Nathan, laughin' at my reaction, responded, "We'll make sure the constable don't find out nothin'. Even if he suspects somethin', there's nothin' he can prove."

Jacob spoke for the first time, "Mr. Jack," he said softly, "Let me show you somethin'." He pulled down his overall straps over each shoulder and took off his ragged shirt and turned his back to me. Large, black welts were all across his back where he'd been beaten. He put his shirt back on and buckled his overall straps.

"I shore would do anythin' I could do for you maybe someday down the road if 'in you'd try to help," stated Jacob.

That about did it for me. Suddenly, I was as mad as scared. "Okay, Nathan," I said. "I'll see Mr. C. D. Tummond first thing Monday mornin'. Do I tell him this is your idea or that I'm in this all alone? Just what do I tell him?"

Nathan responded softly, "Don't let your emotions git the best of you. Better to talk to Mr. C.D. in a calm manner.

Those Were the Times

You can tell him I'm involved if he first agrees to keep all you tell him to himself. Don't tell him where Abraham and Jacob are hid. I heard you can take Mr. C.D. for his word. Trouble is, that he's gonna haf to get the manager or one of the owners to go along with this idea. Just maybe they really need some good workers right now. I hear they are tryin' to git some workers out of the state prison. The prison may release a few to 'em if they have a job. So far, I ain't ever heard of the lumber mill abusin' workers. They just pay 'em as damn little as they can then try to git it all back."

As I started to leave, I was surprised when Abraham and Jacob came over and gave me a hug. God shore made each of 'em big with a powerful build. I also noticed somethin' else for sure. They both desperately needed some clean clothes.

"Nathan," I said as he was leavin'. "You also need a plan to get Abraham and Jacob a bath, maybe some sweet smellin' lotion, and some clean clothes."

The men laughed as I left to return to the Commissary Store and talk to C.D. again. Nathan wanted me to talk to him as quick as possible. I got scared again as I made my way to the Commissary Store. My mind was pourin' over all the ways I was gonna get in trouble over the things I tell C.D., and thinkin' of those two poor colored people back in the woods. They had to be eaten up by mosquitoes, ticks, red bugs, and other bitin' critters.

I got back to the Commissary Store just after noon. C.D. had just returned from dinner. His house was close to the Commissary Store. C.D. was talkin' to one of the laborers who wanted a little advance money. He wanted four dollars in advance, and since he was a good worker, C.D. gave him three dollars. Actually, he really only wanted two dollars but he knew that C.D. would give him a little less than he asked for.

"Jack," C.D. said with a surprised look, "You caught that mess of fish already?"

"No sir," I replied. "I got some might serious talkin' to do with you, and, it's got to be totally confidential. You gotta swear not to tell nobody 'bout this."

"Okay," replied C.D. "You got my word."

He got up from his desk and shut his office door.

I carefully explained the situation and Nathan's plan. "Nathan said to tell you these two colored men are really good workers."

C.D. didn't immediately respond. He sat very quietly lookin' out his side window and then down at his shoes and finally at me.

"Jack," C.D. responded quietly. "You could be backin' our bare asses into a hornet's nest. Some of 'em turpentine people are meaner than hell, and you know they got the law on their side with 'em colored men owin' money. Did they say what turpentine still they worked for?"

"They told Nathan it was just a turpentine still." I replied. "They said the deputy's name was Dan Jones and the turpentine man with him was named Ben Smith. They said Ben Smith was in charge of the Commissary Store and also boss of the workers. He went after any workers who tried to run away still owin' the store money."

"I know the owner," responded C.D. "And I know of Ben Smith. Folks say he is a rough character. Best to stay out of his way. I guess he was the one that strapped Jacob. I'll talk to one of the mill owners and try to work out somethin'. We do need some laborers right now. Did they say how much they owed the turpentine still Commissary Store?"

"I think they told Nathan that one of 'em owed about twenty-five dollars and the other owed about fourteen dollars," I replied.

"Jack," C.D. responded. "I'll talk to the mill manager and one of the owners today, and if they say okay, I'll call the owner of the turpentine still. I'll tell him we hired these two fellows and find out how much money they owe and offer to pay it off. I don't think he will fight over it, but I wouldn't be surprised if the deputy and Ben Smith don't show up and find out who put us up to hirin' these fellas and maybe how they got here. You better be mighty careful. If they found out that you were involved in helpin' 'em two colored men, then I wouldn't be surprised if Ben Smith tried to teach you a lesson. They also may find out about Nathan, but I ain't worryin' 'bout him. I wouldn't advise nobody to bother Nathan Curney but they may try. Why don't you check with me on Monday, and I'll tell you what the situation is with 'em two fellas. Be sure and tell Nathan exactly what I've told you."

"I will," I quickly responded. "I'll go back by and let Nathan know this afternoon."

I walked south, back to Nathan's house along side of Highway 19/98. As I walked, I continued to think about the kind of trouble I could be in and how bad the situation may become for Nathan and those two run-away turpentine workers.

Suddenly, I thought about my Dad. If that deputy and Ben Smith found out about me, they could end up at my house and get Dad involved. I became scared again. I began to tell myself I had to stop thinkin' about this mess. It surely was beginnin' to ruin the peaceful week I had planned.

Nathan's wife greeted me once again. She was sweepin' off the front porch when I arrived.

"Jack," she said with a smile. "This is two times on the same day! I'll call Nathan.

Before she could call, Nathan walked out of the house onto the porch.

"Good to see you back so soon," Nathan said. "Let's sit on the porch and talk. My wife knows 'bout our problem."

I carefully explained the conversation I had with C.D. Tummond and then told Nathan I was worryin' about the trouble I may get into and even maybe my dad. I emphasized what C.D. said about the deputy and Ben Smith and that he'd heard Ben Smith was a bad man. C.D. had said that's prob'ly who beat Jacob and maybe other workers who tried to escape owin' 'em money. I could see that Nathan was deeply concerned.

"Jack," Nathan said in a determined voice. "You let me do the worryin' 'bout Ben Smith or anyone else comin' to the hammock to beat up on somebody. When they cross that Suwannee River bridge headin' this way, they are in our woods. When you chase the chaser, and the chaser's in his own woods, you're gonna get caught."

I could suddenly see a dangerous glint in Nathan's eye, and his voice had an edge of steel. I had not ever seen him in this mood, and I was glad I was on his side in this situation. I felt better. I didn't know anyone that was more than a match for Nathan and especially in the hammock.

"You take care," said Nathan. "And quit that worryin' for a while."

I left Nathan's house and headed for home. I went through the short-cut by Aunt Liza. When I passed the dim trail that led to the pond where Abraham and Jacob were hid, I thought about goin' in and seein' if they were there. I decided not to and continued on home.

I did enjoy the peace and quiet of an all day fishin' trip on Sunday. I caught a number of shell crackers and five good size bass. I cleaned the fish on Sunday afternoon, and my dad fried the fish and made some hush puppies. I didn't think I'd ever meet anybody who could cook and fry fish and hush puppies as good as my dad.

I dropped off a good mess of fish for Mr. C.D. Tummond. He wasn't home, so I left 'em with his next door neighbor, Mr. Horriston. He said he'd take half and give C.D. the other half. I told him that was fine since I had more than enough for both families. Mr. Horriston said he was just jokin' but I found out later that he did decide to keep half.

On Monday mornin', I went by to see Mr. C.D. who was at his office when I arrived.

"Jack," said C.D. with a smile. "I got the fish and I did notice they were cleaned. We're havin' a fish fry tonight."

There was no one waitin' to see Mr. C.D., so we had a chance to talk.

"Jack," said C.D. "I did call the owner of the turpentine still and got an okay from our manager and one of the owners said to play it by ear. I told the owner that we'd hired those two workers and had found out they owed 'em some money and we'd pay it off. He wasn't too happy 'bout the situation, but agreed if we paid 'em off. It ended up costin' us 'bout forty dollars. It'll take those two a while to work that off. He said his son may stir up a little ruckus over this and may have the support of their local deputy. I told him I thought we could handle it if they tried to cause some trouble. We need to get these colored men here this mornin'. I'm turnin' 'em over to the quarter's boss and have him get 'em a place to live and to put the word out in the colored quarters to kinda look out for these two. Maybe keep 'em out of sight 'til all this blows over. They will be workin' in the loggin' woods, and the foreman said he'd look after 'em. Now, Jack. You best not come here with 'em, but tell 'em to wait by the back of Aunt Liza's house, and I'll pull up my car beside her house. They need to come with me back to the office. I'll do their paperwork and the quarter's boss will take it from there. I don't want you or Nathan seen with 'em two."

"Should I go now and see Nathan and get 'em two up back of Aunt Liza's?" I asked.

"Yes," C.D. responded. "But keep out of sight. By the way, you got a job at the lumber yard startin' Monday mornin'. Get there a little early and see Mr. Slay."

Things were beginnin' to look good to me as I walked along the side of the highway on my way to Nathan's house. Thank God Nathan was home! I quickly told him about the conversation I had with C.D.

Nathan responded with a smile and said, "Jack, let's go get Abraham and Jacob."

To my surprise, they were not where I last saw them. Nathan had moved 'em to another nearby location. I didn't think anybody would have even found 'em there.

"Nathan," I asked. "You didn't trust me knowin' where they were?"

"Jack," Nathan replied softly. "I completely trust you but you can't tell somethin' you don't know about. I hope you can understand that."

To my surprise, both Abraham and Jacob had on new overalls, denim shirts, and brogan shoes. They both had even shaved.

"Nathan," I said in a surprised voice. "These ain't the two fellas I met Saturday. Who are these two?"

Both Abraham and Jacob had a big smile. Nathan quickly explained the situation to them, and Abraham began to repeat "Praise the Lord, praise the Lord!" He hugged Jacob, then Nathan, and then I got my turn. Then Jacob started his round of hugs.

Nathan said, "We'd better git the hell outta here and git up back of Aunt Liza's."

They all moved quickly, and as soon as they got to Aunt Liza's, C.D. pulled up in his car. Nathan and I stayed back in the edge of the woods while Abraham and Jacob ran and got in C.D's car. C.D. backed the car up and headed toward the Commissary Office. Nathan and I stood in silence watchin' C.D. pull out of sight.

Nathan put his arm around my shoulder and with a big smile said, "Well, Jack, I think we have won round one, and if there's another round, come hell or high water, we're gonna win that one, too! The fight's over, and we sure as hell won it all even if it's only for Abraham and Jacob. Lots more battles down this road for lots of other folks."

"You know, Nathan," I replied. "I don't think I can handle any more battles. I'm gonna have a heart attack or nervous breakdown if I have many more days like the last three!"

Nathan laughed and responded, "Why don't we go back to my house and sit on the porch and drink a cold Pepsi? If there's another problem, we'll face it when it comes. You're too young for heart attacks!"

We went on to Nathan's house, had a cold Pepsi and I started walkin' toward home. I began to think about Nathan referrin' to round one that we had just won which led me to think that Nathan did anticipate a round two—which he referred to as maybe a final round. Deep down, I knew this situation was not over and that it was still dangerous. I was to discover I was right the comin' Wednesday mornin'.

Tuesday was a really good day. I fished some that mornin', helped my mother with her weekly washin' of clothes, and helped my dad Tuesday afternoon to weed the garden. On Wednesday mornin' I stopped by the Commissary Store to pick up a Pepsi and some crackers on my way to a good fishin' area along the Waccasassa River. C.D. happened to be in the store.

"Jack," I'm surprised you are this late gettin' to some good fishin' spots," said C.D. "I'll walk out on the porch with you and have a little talk."

I sensed somethin' was botherin' him as we walked out on the Commissary porch and set down on one of the long benches.

"Jack," C.D. said in a concerned voice. "I had a talk with Perry Osteen, our local constable yesterday, and he told me that Ben Smith and a deputy were in the area yesterday. They talked with Perry and were interested in knowin' who might have helped 'em two run-away colored men git in contact with us and had maybe helped 'em git to this area. Ben Smith told Perry that if other niggers workin' for his Pa's company heard about this, then they may try to run away and come here knowin' some people around here would help. He felt he needed to put a stop to people around here helpin' runaways.

Mr. C.D. continued, "I called his father, the company owner and our Levy County Sheriff. The turpentine company owner said he told his son that this was finished business, and he didn't want him here stirrin' up problems but he added that Ben was a real hot head. Our sheriff called the deputy that was with Ben and told him he had no jurisdiction or business

Stories by Jack Foley

in Levy County. He also called the County Sheriff where the turpentine still is located and inquired about his deputy comin' here. He told the Sheriff if anythin' needed investigatin' in Levy County to let him know and he'd take care of it. I don't think the deputy will be comin' back, but I'd bet Ben Smith will."

I thanked Mr. C.D. for the information and decided to head toward Nathan's and fished a small creek just north of his house. Nathan wasn't there when I went by so I left word with his wife that I'd come back by later in the day. I felt sure that Ben Smith would be comin' back. When I returned from fishin', Nathan was home.

"I see that big string of fish you got," said Nathan as I walked up to this porch. "I'll help you clean 'em for half."

"That's a deal," I said quickly with a smile.

Nathan's wife was standin' in the front door listenin' to our conversation.

"Jack," she said. "Why don't you stay a while, and I'll cook up a fish fry?"

"I'd do that," I replied. "But Dad planned on me gettin' home for a fish fry this evenin'. I'll sure stay another time if I'm invited."

She brought out two Pepsi's, and me and Nathan sat on the porch and talked. I told Nathan what Mr. C.D. had told me regardin' the Abraham and Jacob situation. Nathan listened intently to everythin' I told him. He sat quietly for a few minutes. Nathan seemed to be in deep thought.

"Jack,' Nathan finally said. "I guess this is gonna be round two and has to be the last round. Whatever happens, I want you to never repeat a word of this talk." I was never more concerned than I was now.

It was the comin' Saturday mornin' that I got another severe shock to my whole system. My heart was beatin' so hard that I couldn't swallow. I stayed shaky that entire weekend. I was just leavin' the house on Saturday when Mr. C.D. pulled his car up along side of me .

"Want a ride to the Commissary Store?" asked C.D.

"Sure," I replied. "I wasn't exactly goin' that way, but I'll stop there and get a cold drink."

I got in the car and we headed toward the Commissary Store. We got to the store, and Mr. C.D. asked me to come into his office. We went in and he closed the door. I knew somethin' had gone wrong.

"Jack," C.D. began. "I don't know how to tell you this, but Ben Smith is in critical shape in the hospital over in Gainesville. They think he will live but he is in bad shape. Both his hands are busted up. Looks like somebody stomped on 'em. He has a fractured skull and some busted ribs."

"What happened," I asked in shock.

"Don't know for sure," said C.D. "The Levy County Sheriff and the Sheriff from the county where the turpentine still is located, are investigatin' the matter. The most I have learned is someone contacted Ben Smith by phone and would not identify himself. Told Ben Smith he knew 'bout who helped 'em colored men escape into Levy County and get a job. Told Ben he hated niggers and he'd give him the information he needed if he'd meet him this past Friday night on the grade that goes from Highway 19/98 to Williams Landin'. Asked him to come alone as he didn't want anyone else to know him. Ben told his deputy friend about this but insisted he go alone. A couple of men goin' fishin' found Ben in the ditch late Friday night. That's about all I know."

I sat in silence for a few minutes. I believed both Mr. C.D. and me were thinkin' the same thoughts even though we never talked about those thoughts...Nathan Curney had said this was round two and it was the end of the fight.

The investigation lasted only a brief period of time and was dropped. To my knowledge no one from that turpentine still ever showed back up in Gulf Hammock. I still think of the plans I had for a really good, peaceful and relaxed week before goin' to work at the mill that summer. I found out from Dad that the lumber yard foreman had a job for me that started early Monday mornin'. At least that was a high note to all the stress I'd gone through.

Stories by Jack Foley

The Author's Historic Note

Florida's first convict leasing statute was passed in 1877. This authorized counties to lease their convicts to private firms.

On January 1, 1905, there was a "public outcry" from a representative of Levy County convicts. The message was "The Levy County convicts will be offered for hire to the highest bidder. All convicts will be in the custody of the highest bidder for the year beginning January 1, 1905, and ending December 1, 1905."

The Author's Comment:

There was an article in the Levy County Journal of the possible mistreatment of these prisoners. It is entirely possible that this article was ignored by certain law enforcement personnel.

The Author's Historic Note

In 1919, the state was prohibited from leasing convicts to private firms. However, the leasing continued until the horrible beating death of Martin Tabert, a young man from South Dakota. The brutal beating was inflicted by the "whipping Boss" (Walter Higginbotham) at one of the turpentine camps owned by the Putnam Lumber Company.

This brutal event shed national notoriety on Dixie County and led to state and national legislative action. The ensuing legislation passed in 1923 ended this long-standing abusive practice.

The Author's Comment:

This is a tragic example of corruption at every level. There have been a number of articles and a book published about this tragedy.

Those Were the Times

Chapter 7

Humor and Tragedy

The very first week I was paid as a stick boy, I was pleasantly surprised. The money was significantly more than I had made either of the last two summers. I was told there was a change made for minimum wages and a stick boy's salary was placed under the minimum wage law. That was good news!

I was up early on Monday and walked with Dad through the boardwalk to the mill. I was supposed to work with Dad but Will Safford had asked if I could work with him for a couple of weeks on the Green Chain. Will Safford and Felix greeted me. Will Safford asked me to go down the Green Chain and pull all pine boards that were two inches thick, eight inches wide, and ten feet long with the lumber buggy directly across from a black woman named Dora.

I went down the Green Chain until I was across from Dora. I thought, at first she was a man. She had a rather large, stocky build and was dressed in men's overalls, a denim shirt, men's brogan shoes, and had a large, red handkerchief wrapped around the top of her head.

I spoke to her and told her my name and that Will Safford and Felix had sent me down to pull the two inch by eight inch by ten foot pine boards into the buggy across from her. She barely noticed. I looked over at the boards in her buggy, and it looked like she was pullin' two by ten by twelve inch pine boards—a little bit larger boards than mine. I had never pulled green lumber off the Green Chain.

My experience in pullin' lumber with buggies was dry lumber in the Planer Mill. I was in for a major shock! I saw some of the lumber I was to pull comin' down the Green Chain, and I got ready to pull.

I moved up about six feet ahead of my buggy and got a two hand grip about two feet up the board and began to move down toward my buggy. I was ready! I could easily pull it into my buggy. I pulled, and the board did not move! I pulled with all my strength and it did not budge! Now the board was passin' the buggy, and more boards were followin'.

I was about to panic when I heard Dora laughin' and then she hollered, "White boy, you best let all dem boards go and run back up hea and start wif dem comin' up to yo buggy. Let dem others drop off at the end of the Green Chain. I'll hep you catch up hea. Let's start wif dem comin' up to yo buggy."

I ran back up just beyond my buggy to make a second attempt at pullin' green lumber. Dora was already there. She had crossed over the Green Chain on to my side. She said she didn't see any of her lumber comin' at the moment.

"Look hea, white boy," said Dora. "Don't try to pull dem boards straight off. First move the end of the board from side to side on the Green Chain. Dat will break its grip the turpentine has on the cables. Git it movin' to and fro and at the same time as you move it, pull toward you. Hit'll start movin' toward the buggy. Den you start to bear down and pull it toward the empty buggy. You jus watch me."

I carefully watched Dora, and she made it seem so easy that I was embarrassed. In a few practices, I could pull the lumber into the buggy but not as easy as Dora made it look. Dora crossed back over the Green Chain as some of her lumber was close.

On our first break, I went over to Dora's side to thank her. I tried to give her a hug, but she would not cooperate. She told me to git myself on my side of the Green Chain and to behave myself. I told her (in good humor!) that I'd save the hug for later.

Dora then told me that I had a much bigger problem. "You need to load all your boards that fell off the end of the Green Chain after work."

After work, I ran down to the end of the Green Chain. There were about ten boards that I would need to get loaded in my buggy.

As I was lookin' at this heavy lumber, I saw Slim Paget comin' up from the lumber yard pullin' an empty lumber buggy. Except for Dora, I have never been happier to see anyone! I just knew he would help me. I started hollerin' and tryin' to wave him down.

He pulled up close to me and I explained my problem. He really laughed when I told him how it happened. We loaded up, and I ran up to my lumber buggy by the Green Chain.

Dora was still there, and she told Slim what happened. She said it was a bad joke that was played on me.

"That white boy ain't never pulled that kind of lumber off the Green Chain, and I bet Will Safford is up there still laughin'! I kinda doubt Felix sees anythin' funny about this. If he didn't laugh a little, he could lose his job with Will Safford."

The mill whistle sounded at that moment markin' the end of the work day. As I crossed over by the Planer Mill, I noticed a small group of workers gathered to listen to one of Roosevelt's stories. There were a number of Negro story tellers at the mill, and Roosevelt and his accomplice, Chevrolet, were the most popular.

Roosevelt is always the big hero of his stories, and his best friend, Chevrolet, is always involved by repeating comments at different parts of Roosevelt's stories.

Roosevelt begins, "I ain't gotta work at this ol' mill! I bin gitten a good pension from my workin' for the FBI!"

"Ooo," injects Chevrolet. "Dats a lie! He ain't ever bin wif no FBI!"

Roosevelt paid no attention to Chevrolet and continued.

"Couple of years ago, the head man of the FBI called for me and said Roosevelt, we got a real bad man runnin' all over robbin' banks, trains, beatin' up on men, molestin' women, and he's the meanest man ever lived. You gotta come back and now! You are the onlyiest one that always got yo man. Ain't nobody 'cept you that can handle this. We need you back as fast as you can git here."

"Oooh, oooh, what a lie," responded Chevrolet as he walked around the crowd lookin' down and kickin' up small piles of dirt. "He ain't got no phone!"

By now, the small crowd was fully into Roosevelt's story. They were clappin' hands and laughin'. Chevrolet's antics were addin' to the laughter. Roosevelt paid no attention to Chevrolet.

He continued, "I got up a few of my belongs and jumped on the trail of that mean rascal. I almost caught him up in Georgia. I done chased him all 'round cotton and watermelon fields. He tried to hide out at this little farm house wif some ugly old Georgia woman. All she wanted to do was some romancin' and eat watermelon. Even bof at the same time!

"What a lie!" shouted Chevrolet. "He ain't never knowed no Georgia women and he ain't never even gone as far as Otter Creek which is six miles up the road. He sho do knows some ugly women here!"

"Anyway," continued Roosevelt. "Dat ugly ol woman come outta de house wif a shotgun and most blowed me away. I had to run fer my life. She helped dat scandrel git away. It took some time for me to pick up his trail again. It took days to chase him all the way to Canadie where I joined up wif the Royal Mounties."

"Ooo,ooo," shouted Chevrolet. "I done tol you he ain't never ben as far as Otter Creek. He don't know where Canadie is. He seed them Royal Mounties in the picture show last week."

Stories by Jack Foley

The crowd roared with laughter. Many of them had gone to the weekly movie they have in Gulf Hammock, and it was about the Royal Mounties.

Roosevelt paid no attention to the interruption as he continued.

"I borried a Mountie's horse and kep trackin' that bad man all the way to Alaskes. I had to ride for my life when two of dem big white pollie bears chased me for almost ten miles. They almost caught me and that would have ended my chase of the bad man. I hit out in one of dem ice houses wif an eskimoe 'til dem dam pollie bears gave up and left. I stayed almost a month in the ice house wif dat eskimoe!"

Chevrolet shouted, "Lordy! Lordy! His lies are gittin' bigger and deeper! Ain't nobody can believe two pollie bears chasin' his black ass through the snow!" Chevolet continued to look down and kick up dirt.

The crowd roared with laughter, and there was a lot of knee slappin' and clappin'.

"I got rat back on the trail," Roosevelt continued. "I found my man holed up in a cabin covered wif snow. I saw a small barn beside the house where I could put the Mountie horse. I took the lasso rope off the saddle and went and hid under the edge of the porch."

Chevrolet shouted, as he kicked up a big pile of dirt, "You are now hearin' the biggest lie of all! These lies are huge!"

Roosevelt continued, "I was hid under the edge of the porch for two weeks before that bad man had to have a bowel movement. He came out and started down the steps to go to the bushes when I stepped out with my lasso rope and made a good throw. I had him around the neck. I had my man!" The crowd was wild with laughter and hand clappin'!

When Roosevelt ended his story, I saw Dad leavin' the Planer Mill and headin' for the boardwalk for home. I ran across and caught up with him. I was too tired to do anythin' else but go home, eat supper, and go to bed.

Those Were the Times

I was up early after a good night's sleep and walked the boardwalk with Dad to the mill. When I got to the top of the Green Chain, only Will Safford was there. He knew Felix and I were good friends, and he said he was sorry to break the news to me, but Felix was dead. I could not believe Will Safford! He went on to remind me that almost every afternoon, Felix walked by the Commissary Store and bought an orange soda and sat on an outside bench to enjoy his drink. He was finishin' his drink and had a heart attack and died. The news that a person that I cared for as a friend had died was new to me. All I could do to adjust to the news was withdraw. I asked Will Safford if he could find someone to fill in for me today, and he said he could.

I left the mill and went over to the Maby Baptist Church at the Crate Mill Quarters where Felix attended and at times preached. Just above the church, one of the creeks from the Wekiva Springs made a sharp bend and there was a beautiful place to sit and fish. The water was crystal clear. Sometimes I came here on Sundays and listened to Felix preach. I stayed at the creek the remainder of the day and then left for home.

Dad was already home and had heard about Felix. Will Safford had told him he let me off for the day.

The next mornin' when I got to work, Will Safford had more bad news. He said he was notified that Dora had been arrested and charged with murder. She had shot her husband when he came to the place where he and Dora lived in the Odessa Quarters. It happened sometime after midnight.

Will Safford said I would need to fill in for her until they could git a replacement. I felt numb. Without respondin' to Will Safford, I headed down the Green Chain to Dora's area and prepared to pull boards. I was lucky as the boards were only eight footers.

At around nine o'clock, I was in for a big surprise. Mr. CD Tummond pulled up by the Green Chain and Dora got out of his car. He had brought her there from the office. Someone from the Sheriff's Office in Bronson had brought her to the lumber mill offices.

I was told the day after Dora was arrested that one of the owners of the lumber company visited the judge and the charge of murder was changed to justifiable homicide. There was a fine of $25 for court costs.

I told Dora how glad I was to see her—especially before any two by twelve by tens came my way! Dora and I became friends. She quit callin' me "White Boy" and called me Jack. I later learned that Dora's husband had been abusive to her.

I thought of Felix and his stories often and especially one of the last stories he had told.

Felix began, "Always remember the message of the story. The message is what's important."

> "A rich, young white man wanted to learn to be a big game hunter and kill big tigers. He went to Africa and hired a young guide that knowed all about huntin' and killin' big tigers. He tol the young guide dem tigers he wanted to kill were a special kind a tiger and they weren't many survivin'. The guide said he didn't care none, long as he gits paid lots of money to kill 'em. The rich young white man paid the guide lots of money. On the first huntin' trip, the guide found where one of them special big tigers were hid. The guide warned the young man that when they got close to where the tiger was hid that the tiger would charge. He tol the young man to move up front and let the big cat charge and when he got close, then shoot him. The young man moved slowly up toward where the tiger was hid.
>
> The big cat charged, and the young man did not bring his gun up quick enough. The guide was watchin' and shot the big tiger before it reached the young man. The guide shouted, 'I done tol you dat you needed to get

real good at Quick Shots In Short Distances!' They went back to camp and the young man started each mornin' by gettin' good at taking quick shots in short distances.

Somethin' strange begins to happen. Each time he would practice, there would be lots of noise a short distance off in the brush. When the young man would stop each practice shot, the noise would stop. This started to worry the young hunter. He would stop his practice and walk around the area where he heard the noise, but he would never see or hear anythin'. He thought of a trick. He would git one of the natives from the huntin' party to sneak out in the brush and hide, and he started his practice. Sho nuff, the noise would start with each practice shot and then stop.

The young hunter stopped and called for the native to come out. The native came out with a surprised look. 'What the hell is out there?' asked the young hunter. 'Suh, hits hard to believe, but there's one of dem rare, big tiger cats practicin' Quick Jumps in Short Distances!'

The crowd roared with laughter, and Felix stood with a solemn look. As the crowd quieted down, he told them, "It's mighty hard for poor folks to survive durin' these hard times, and we all need to learn how to make quick jumps in mighty short distances!"

Chapter 8

Frolics and Revivals

There are events in the hammock that will lift the spirits and certain ones provide for never endin' gossip that become myths. It becomes difficult to separate fact from fiction since each time the stories are told, they are embellished by the storyteller to make 'em even more interestin'!

Events include church services, cane grindin', peanut boilin', huntin', and fishin' camp parties, square dances, and frolics.

Frolics were mostly considered undesirable events dependin' somewhat on where they were held and who attended. The frolics I came to know 'bout and the ones I attended was considered somewhat typical.

The typical frolic generally started early on Saturday mornin' or late on Friday evenin'. The frolic ended on Sunday mornin' when some folk begin to wake up and begin to learn to walk again. Some had bad hangovers. When I say bad, I have been told there is nothin' worse than a sick moonshine or red liquor hangover! The moonshine is homemade, and the red liquor is illegally sold at a price most folk can afford.

No question that some frolics attracted what most of the regular church goin' folk of the town of Gulf Hammock referred to as sorry-good-for-nothin' heathens who are bound straight for hell! The preacher described hell in such vivid terms that you could actually feel the heat from the fire, smell the brimstone, and hear the cryin' out in great pain from all the heathen frolickers who had passed away.

In spite of the great pain and horror described by the preacher, there were still folk who had a greater and more immediate need to raise their spirits up several notches higher by full participation in frolics and other such events. Most, if not all, thought there would still be plenty of time after goin' to the frolics to git right with Jesus and ride that train to glory. They would be right there with all the good church goin' folk who had missed out on the frolics and certain other spirit liftin' undesirable events.

However, they know for a fact that certain ones of the supposedly good God fearin' Christians had not missed out on the frolics and other undesirable events. It was a small minority of those who attended church who also attended frolics. Nonetheless, it was well known that "ladies of the night" attended certain frolics.

Durin' huntin' season, a few men from huntin' camps would show up at frolics and fully participate.

The more I learned about frolics, the more I wanted to attend. I felt my chance came when I learned that my older brother, Fred's, band would be providin' music for a certain frolic. This was a surprise! I also thought it would be a surprise to Mother and Dad. It was also a surprise for me to learn that there were some people from surroundin' towns in Levy County who attended local frolics.

I could hardly wait to see Fred, and maybe there was a chance he'd let me go with him. I knew my chance was slim, and I also knew I would have to threaten to tell Mother and Dad everythin' I knew about Fred that I had collected over time that he may prefer they didn't know.

When Fred got home late Sunday evenin', I was anxious to talk. I finally got my chance when he went out on the front porch to sit down on the porch swing. I came out quickly to sit down beside him. I made sure I didn't interfere with how he wanted to move the swing.

"Fred," I began, "I hear you are goin' to play for a frolic this comin' Saturday and it will last 'til Sunday."

"Where did you hear that?" Fred asked quickly.

Stories by Jack Foley

"I found out from a friend of mine from Otter Creek. His brother went to a dance you played for recently. His brother plans to go to the frolic," I said. I was bein' very polite in the way I was approachin' my request because Fred has a quick temper, and I was hopin' not to make him mad.

"This frolic thing is just talk. There is always talk about where we will play next," said Fred. "Besides, you, Joe, and Bull always go to the square dance out in Inglis on Saturday night."

"I really want to go to the frolic, and I could skip the square dance. I know some boys younger than me that go to the frolic," I responded.

"The answer is no. I don't think Mom or Dad would be too happy if you went to a certain frolic," Fred sternly replied.

"No more happy to learn that you play for frolics and fully participate in 'em with the worst of reputations," I said. "Besides, I could be spendin' the weekend with the Berryhills. Mother and Dad ain't concerned about my comins' and goins'." I added, "There are some other things I could tell Mother and Dad."

I could tell Fred was gettin' angry, and I was gettin' a little scared. He had me trapped in the swing. I felt I was in a dangerous situation.

Fred glared at me for a short time and then said thoughtfully, "There are some things you had better not do and some things you had better do if I let you go. Number one is you better not git in no fight. Number two is you had better stay within my sight all the time we are there. Number three is you had better not drink nothin' but water. Number four, you are not to tell anybody that you were there or of anythin' that happened."

I quickly said, "I can handle old number four and all the other numbers and if you think of a five or six, I can handle 'em also!"

Fred looked at me with a long, thoughtful look and finally responded. "Yes, somethin' down deep is tellin' me that this is a big mistake, so yes, there is a five or six."

I quickly responded, "I can handle them. What are they?"

Fred looked at me hard and responded, "Five is I'll never loan my car to you again for you and the Berryhill boys to look for females to court or to go to that square dance in Inglis and six is that I'm gonna beat your bony ass on a regular basis."

Since Fred was not smilin' but had a hard, scary look, I knew I was goin' to abide by all his numbers, and again I assured him of my very best behavior.

Fred plays a lead guitar, Ralph plays rhythm guitar. Peck Watson plays a bass fiddle and sometimes a wanderin' fiddle player and storyteller named Cush Holsome pops in. They all grew up 'round the town of Gulf Hammock except Cush who grew up around Cedar Key.

I could hardly wait to see and hear that band play. I heard they were really good.

Fred and I left 'round noon on Saturday mornin', and I still did not know where we were goin'.

Fred, I asked, "Where is this frolic?"

"Do you know where the old Tindale place is?" answered Fred.

"Yes," I replied. "Ain't it on the Lebanon Grade close to Cow Creek?"

"That's it," Fred said. "It's a large frame house and it has a rather large front room. The frolic will begin outside the house and move into the front room about dark. The dancin' and story tellin' will begin when we move inside. Cush will do most of the story tellin' and Will Long will call the square dancin'."

Fred added, "Now one thing for sure, remember the things I told you or I'll send you packin' back through the woods home."

I responded quickly, "I remember everythin' you told me and you can count on me! What about food? We didn't bring nothin' to eat."

"Don't worry," Fred responded. "They have someone roastin' a couple of wild hogs as well as preparin' other food. There will be people bringin' food. There will be lots of food."

We stopped by and picked up Ralph Cobb and Peck Watson. It was really crowded with me and all the instruments in the small back seat. The three of 'em were in the front seat.

I didn't dare complain. Fred was not beyond puttin' me out.

We went out close to Wekiva Springs and turned north on Lebanon Grade to the Tindale place. The Tindale place was a large frame house with a porch around three quarters of the house. The livin' room was really large. It was if the builder planned for havin' frolics.

There were 'round ten or more people already there. Some were roastin' two hogs while others were helpin' prepare for the frolic.

I noticed some were preparin' early by sippin' what I assumed was moonshine.

Marge Tindale came out and greeted Fred and the other band members and introduced her other female friends. She looked at me as I was gettin' out of the car.

"Fred," Marge said with a big smile. "Who is this good lookin' young man you brought along?"

"That's my younger brother," replied Fred. "He can help out with any chores you need done. His name is Jack."

"Well now, Jack," Marge said with smile and lookin' me over closely. "I think you can be real useful. I got a couple of good lookin' young ladies comin' by to see me. They are my sisters' girls. They will be pleased to have someone their age to visit with."

"Yes, ma'am," I responded. "I'll help anyway I can. I would be pleased to meet the young ladies."

Fred and the band members began to set up to play under a huge old oak tree by the side of the house. They planned to move inside at dark.

While they were settin' up to play, I heard a lot of shoutin' and loud fiddle music playin' off at a distance.

As the sounds drew closer and louder, I saw it was a large flatbed Model A truck with about twelve or fourteen people ridin' on the bed of the truck. It was stomp down great fiddle music. It had to be Cush Holsome. The whole group was makin' one whale of a noise as they piled out of the truck. I noticed two young teenage girls gettin' out. They were most likely Mrs. Tindale's kin. I would know soon.

Cush Holsome, while laughin' and jokin', got together with Fred and the other band members. They were all enjoyin' getting' together again.

I went over and sat down on the edge of the front porch. I was really enjoyin' watchin' all the folk there, talkin' and jokin' with each other.

The two teenage girls I saw get off the flatbed truck came over to the edge of the porch where I was and started a conversation with me. It would be a stretch of the truth to say they were real pretty, but fair to say they were both very shapely and looked good!

However, I will also tell you that before that night was over that I honestly believed those two girls could be the death of me or lead to a near death experience provided by my brother, Fred.

They were not Marge Tindale's kin but came with an uncle from Tidewater. Them two knew and used more cuss words than I had ever heard and I thought I knew a lot!

"What's your name?" the older of the two sisters asked.

"Jack," I replied. "What's yours?"

"Annie," she said. "And this is my sister, Bobbie Jo."

"What's yo last name?" asked Bobbie Jo.

Before I could answer, Annie responded, "His last name is Ass so his whole name is Jack Ass."

Both girls started laughin' and Bobbie Jo continued to poke more fun about my name. As far as I was concerned, their funnin' had gone far enough.

"Why don't you two little morons go find somethin' useful to do or at least try and just be seen and not heard?" I responded with a touch of anger.

"Ain't no need to git mad," said Annie. "When they start playin' some music, we'll do some dancin' with you. That outta' make you happy."

"It'll take more than a little dancin' with either of you to make me happy." I responded.

Fred called for me to come over where the band was gettin' ready to play.

"You gonna play in that band?" asked Bobbie Jo excitedly.

"No," I replied. "That's my brother's band and I do chores for him."

"Can me and Annie come over and meet your brother and the other ones that play with him?" asked Bobbie Joe.

"Sure, but don't smart off!" I replied as we went over to see what Fred wanted. I introduced him and the other band members to Annie and Bobbie Jo. Fred wanted me to go get some guitar picks he'd left in the glove box of the car but mostly I think he wanted me to know he was aware of my where abouts.

I brought back Fred's picks and began to pay a little more attention to Annie and Bobbie Jo as they were talkin' with the band members. They looked enough alike to almost be twins. Both had full lips, bright blue eyes, and reddish brown hair pulled back in pony tails. They were real lively and began to look even better than my first impression. No matter though, I somehow knew those two could cause me a heap of trouble. While they were visitin' with the band members, their uncle came over. His name was Bossie Strong.

"Okay," said Bossie with a big smile. "I'm supposed to protect you girls from music makers."

"Most folk need to be protected from you," Annie responded. "We can take care of ourselves."

You could tell that he could cause some trouble. He was a rough lookin', loud talkin' character.

I walked back over and set back down on the edge of the porch. It was a good place for a view of the whole front area. I noticed a small group of men, women, and a boy and girl about my age walkin' up to the house.

They had been fishin' down at Cow Creek which was close by. By six o'clock, there were more than thirty-five people there and more comin'. One group brought a large container of green peanuts and wanted to start 'em boilin' for eatin' later in the evenin'. The hogs were cooked so the peanuts could boil over the hot coals used to roast the hogs.

Marge didn't have enough salt for the peanuts and asked around for somebody to go to Lebanon Station and pick up salt at Henry Horne's place. Marge asked me if I could drive. I told her I could, but I did have to ask Fred as I knew he'd said I'd have to stay in sight. Marge said she'd ask, and to my surprise, Fred said okay.

I was walkin' toward the car when I heard someone call out.

"Where you goin'?" asked Annie.

"I'm goin' to Henry Horne's place at Lebanon Station to pick up some salt," I called back.

"Wait up," hollered Bobbie Jo. "We're gonna go with 'ya."

Both came runnin' toward the car, and I could see Fred lookin' in my direction. I gave him the high sign hopin' it would send a message that all was okay. I knew better.

I got in the car as Annie and Bobbie Jo jumped in, with Bobbie Jo in the middle. She was jam up close beside me. I could feel the warmth of her body pressed up against me. I began to get a pleasant feelin' from the warmth.

This was goin' to be an eight mile, slow round trip as the Lebanon Grade was sandy and hard to get through in certain spots. About a half mile from Marge's house, Bobbie Joe pressed her leg closer against mine and put her foot on top of mine causin' me to press down harder on the accelerator. The harder I pulled up foot, the harder she pushed down forcing' me to go faster.

"Jack, you better slow down," stated Annie. "You gonna wreck this car."

"Bobbie Jo," I quickly said, "Git yo damn foot off mine and now!"

"Quit pushin' down on his foot," said Annie. "Think of somethin' else to do besides causin' a damn accident."

Bobbie Jo did think of somethin' else to do and did cause an accident. She pushed down harder! I not only almost died of shock, but lost control of the car and run off the grade into a palmetto patch. As the car went over the edge of the grade and into the palmettos, both Bobbie Jo and Annie were thrown up into the top of the car. Somehow, I managed to use the brakes just enough to stop just before hittin' a big pine tree.

God, Almighty!" I hollered. "What the hell you think you're doin' Bobbie Jo? You could git us all killed!"

"Yea, Bobbie Jo!" shouted Annie. "What the hell you think you're doin?"

"Don't holler at me!" screamed Bobbie Jo. "I know Jack woulda' died happy!"

"That's it!" said Annie. "I'm riding' in the middle the rest of the way."

"Hell no!" I quickly responded. "Both of you are gettin' in the back seat.

"No we ain't!" they both said at the same time as they pushed down hard on my foot causin' the car to lurch forward. Lucky I turned the wheel in time and missed the tree.

"I better check out Fred's car." I said. "He'll kill me for sure if there is even a scratch." I just know he will find out. I must do whatever I can or have to do to git Annie and Bobbie Joe not to tell. My guess is that I will forever be blackmailed.

Good fortune smiled on me for this one time. There was not a scratch, and we backed up onto the grade without gettin' stuck. We went on to Henry Horne's place and picked up the sale without another major crisis. When we started to leave the Horne's place, Annie was sittin' on the driver's side and Bobbie Jo was in the back seat.

"What's goin' on?" I asked with surprise.

Annie replied, "You git in back with Bobbie Joe and I'm gonna drive slow half way back and then I'm gonna get in back with you 'til we git to Cow Creek and then you drive on to the house."

I guess I really did know why Fred didn't want me out of his sight. There's both bad and good trouble to get into and so far this was both kinds, bad and good. Everythin' finally worked out, and we brought back the salt. All I will say is those girls sure knew how to have fun.

The frolic had been quiet up to this point. It was gettin' dark, and now about forty people were there. I noticed that a few of the ladies of the night were also there. Cupie Doll and her sister were there as well as two ladies from the Chiefland area. They surely would pick up a few dollars before the frolic was over.

Right now, things were quieter than I had expected except for my involvement with Annie and Bobbie Jo. Somehow, I knew that Fred was aware that I may be back slidin' on my promises. I noticed he was not talkin' to anyone at the moment so I quickly went over where the band members were.

With a big smile, I asked if I was gettin' a good score. He looked at me for a moment and smiled. Lord, what a relief! Fred told me that he knew the two girls would want me to join in the dancin' and it was alright. At the same time, he warned me of my promises and I best not forget. I went back over and was joined by Annie and Bobbie Jo.

The group enjoyed great food and was ready for music.

Fred asked for quiet and introduced the band members. Then he introduced some extra individuals who showed up and would give individual performances. He introduced a rub board player, a harmonica player, a juice harp player, and a couple who played spoons.

Now, the band was ready.

Cush Holsome held his bow pointin' high in the air. The room was deadly quiet.

Cush hollered, "Hit it!" and the music exploded throughout the room, bounced off the walls and ceilin', flowed through every body and soul, and set the spirits of every frolicker soarin'. Everyone lined up along the wall leavin' the middle of the floor for the dancers. Different groups or individuals would take to the dance floor while the others left along the walls would cheer 'em on. A dance floor manager would direct dancers on and off the floor so everyone had an opportunity to cheer and to dance.

The dance manager called for ten couples to come on the dance floor for a square dance. The caller was Bo Jones.

They were one couple short, and Bobbie Jo ran over and grabbed me. She dragged me out on the floor before I could say squat. Annie insisted I dance with her next.

We formed a circle and was ready for the music. The song was a square dance favorite named "Down Yonder."

The room exploded with the music and the dancers were movin' to the caller and the music. When the caller said all join hands and form a circle, 'ya left the small circle, moved to the left while dancin' to the music. The caller then called for the ladies to drop back one and seven. You git a chance to dance with every lady.

If you don't know how to square dance, you should learn. It's easy to learn!

Everyone got a chance to participate in square dancin'.

At the end of the first square dance, someone hollered, "Cow in the Corn Crib." The music stopped briefly while some folk went out to get a drink of shine and others for different reasons.

When the square dancers finished, the individual performers began. They were great! I went over close to the band and was joined by Annie and Bobbie Jo. I gave up the idea that one or both of 'em would find someone else. There was not much choice of boys in our age group.

The individual performers were great. The first up was a lady who played the spoons and sang "The Wild Wood Flower." There was a lot of cheerin', and she was joined by the juice harp player, and then by a lady called the queen of hambone and then the harmonica player followed by the entire band. All had now joined together playin' and singin' "The Wild Wood Flower."

The crowd was cheerin' and goin' wild. Tom Peterson was sittin' in a chair that was leanin' against a wall. He pulled out a pearl handle pistol and started firin' into the ceilin'.

The music stopped and people scattered in all directions. Henry Horne fell out a window and landed in a wash tub of water. Somebody hollered that more gun shots were comin' toward the house from a wooded area across the Lebanon Grade. Two of the frolickers got shot guns and started shootin' into the wooded area.

The shootin' stopped and the frolickers reorganized. The frolic continued, but without music.

Fred said, "Many of the frolickers had hollered 'Cow in the Corn Crib' too many times." Fred never returned to play for that location again.

Before all the worst happened, I had met with Annie and Bobbie Jo and we had agreed to meet the next Saturday night at the square dance in Inglis. That was close to where they lived. They said their brother would bring them.

Fred told me later that I did okay, but it would be my last frolic with him. That seemed okay with me at the time.

The Author's Historic Note

Congress passed the 18th Amendment to the Constitution in 1919. This was known as the National Prohibition Law which made it illegal to make, sell, import or export any intoxicating beverages.

By 1933, Congress voted to repeal the 18th Amendment. During the rather brief time the 18th Amendment was in place, the nation experienced a national tragedy. There have been many books and movies that include details of this period in our nation's history.

The Author's Comment:

One effect the Prohibition had was to significantly increase the number of moonshiners. The Greater Gulf Hammock area was suspected of having many hidden moonshine stills. I am sure the 18th Amendment was great for the moonshine business! I know of moonshiners and prohibition officers going to weekend frolics together.

Those Were the Times

Chapter 9

A Chance to Win Provides "Hope!"

I learned about Bolita the first summer I worked at Gavin's Grocery Store in Gulf Hammock. Bolita was a lottery that the Mafia operated out of Havana, Cuba in the late 19th, early 20th century. It was called the "little ball lottery." One hundred little balls, numbered 1 to 100, were placed in a bag, mixed thoroughly, and the winning ball was drawn. All bets were made prior to the drawin'. You might be wonderin' if the game can be rigged, and you'd be right—the answer appears to be yes! It is possible that most, if not all, games were rigged.

The game came to Tampa and spread rapidly among the rural workin' white folk including poor blacks and Hispanics. It was amazin' how rapidly the Bolita lottery spread throughout Florida and how the majority of these folks were attracted to this lottery. The Bolita lottery was illegal, but that didn't stop the attraction—probably because the law was not enforced and it was safe to play! It appears that top law enforcement personnel were paid off big time!

Every Saturday afternoon in Cuba, the winnin' number would be given in a broadcast by the Cuban National Lottery. The winnin' number became quickly known wherever Bolita was played. To renew "hope," the process of selectin' a new number or numbers for the comin' Saturday drawin' begins. Some folk played the same number or numbers for every Saturday drawin'. It could be...

The date of the month you got your first kiss...

The date of the month you married your girlfriend or boyfriend...

The date of the month you left your wife or husband...

The date of the month you ran away from home...

The date of the month you ran back home...

The first and only time I played Bolita, I was impressed that it paid "70 to 1"—seventy dollars for a one dollar winnin' lottery ticket! The Bolita number I selected was 26—the day of the month of my birth. I lost! One dollar—and that was my pay for a long, hard day of work! I had to do some serious thinkin' before I invested in another lottery ticket.

I decided one Sunday afternoon that I would forget my loss and go fishin'. I had heard there was a bed of large shell crackers under the beacon light bridge where one of the Wekiva creeks crosses under Highway 19/98. On my way there, I went by Peeks Store and saw my friend, Franklin Schuler.

I told Franklin my "sad" story about my one dollar Bolita loss. He showed no sympathy and asked how I chose my number. When I told him, he said it was a dumb way to pick a lottery number. Not that there is a certain way to pick a winner, but Franklin said there is a way that will improve my chances and told me about a place called "The Satisfaction House."

Franklin said there was a lady there who could read dreams and had other mystic powers to provide a number or numbers for you for just a small fee. The only problem was that Franklin didn't know if she would provide her services to a white person.

He said if she decided to help, she could provide me with a number or numbers that would improve my chance of winnin'. I was very curious and interested in this woman's powers. I asked Franklin about the cost if she agreed to see me. He said she charged fifty cents for the two numbers and ten dollars if I won on either number.

Franklin then smiled and said she may charge me more since I would be a minority customer. He said he would stop by Gavin's Store or come by my house and let me know. I told Franklin I had Sunday and Monday off. I left for my fishin' trip, and Franklin headed for home.

Franklin and some of his friends were swimmin' at the wooden bridge near his house. He stopped me and said he had stopped by the "Satisfaction House" on his way home after talkin' to me. He said he had a time set up—about 8:30 on Monday evenin' and that he would have to go with me—meanin' if I got a number that won, he would get half. I told Franklin at most, he'd get a Pepsi and at least, he'd agree not to ever tell anyone that I set this up.

At 8:30 Monday evenin', we were on our way to the "Satisfaction House." The house was located on a narrow dirt road that went through a wooded area. We went along the side of the house to a side door. Franklin knocked, and a young black girl opened the door, quickly let us in, and closed the door. I could tell that they were takin' care that we would not be seen.

As my eyes adjusted to light in the room, I could see a small table with two chairs across from each other and four candles—one on each corner of the table. There was a tall, attractive lady standin' in back of the table. She had a white, silk turban partially coverin' her hair and a long, silk gown that reached down to the top of white shoes. She smiled and spoke, and I noticed bright white teeth. She looked mystical.

"You're Jack," the lady said. "Yes, ma'am," I replied."

She asked me to sit across from her at the table.

"Franklin asked me for a special favor," she began. "I would be pleased if you would agree to keep our meetin' confidential."

"Yes, ma'am," I said. "I assure you that I will."

"Then we will begin our search for no more than two possible numbers that I may suggest," said the mystical lady. "You do realize there is no guarantee that either number will win?"

"Yes, ma'am," I replied.

"First, I'm going to ask you about one of your most recent dreams. You do sometimes have dreams?" asked the lady.

"Yes, ma'am," I said. "But not very often, and my dreams are usually short and scary. I do remember one dream where I was fishin' up close to Wekiva Springs. I was walkin' through the woods along the river, and I discovered an oak tree that was loaded with fox grapes. The vine was about thirty feet up the tree, and the tree was rather large and it was difficult to climb. I finally made it to the fox grapes. The vines were out on a limb with lots of little branches. It was hard to get to the grapes. They were good, but when I tried to get down the tree, I knew I would fall. It was scary. Then, I remembered that I could fly. I stood up on the limb and dove out over the vines toward the ground. I woke up before I hit the ground and was too scared to go back to sleep!"

"That was a good dream to analyze," she quickly responded. "Now we need one more if possible. Do you possibly remember one more?"

I suddenly remembered dreamin' of gettin' lost in the forty-seven runs swamp, and I was almost panickin'. I felt an urge to run, but I didn't know which way to run. In my dream, a voice of a good friend of mine told me to calm down and "think" my way out. The voice told me to check and see if there was a moon. From that question, I began to use reason and came up with an idea of my location and a possible way out. It worked! In my dream, I was excited as I found my way out! I woke up in a sweat, but I was happy! I guess that is one good dream I had forgotten about.

The lady clapped her hands and asked for everyone to be very quiet. The silence lasted at least half an hour, and then she wrote down two numbers and charged me fifty cents.

It's now been over four months since I got my "enhanced" numbers from the "Satisfaction House." I have not played Bolita and I have noticed neither number has "fell." After losin' my pay for a hard day's work, I gave up on

Bolita. However, I enjoyed my visit to the "Satisfaction House. It somewhat satisfied my curiosity, but I suspect there was much more going on at the "Satisfaction House" than sellin' numbers based on dreams.

It is worth notin' that Bolita ended in 1959 when Fidel Castro led a successful revolution in Cuba, and the Mafia fled.

The Author's Historic Note

The game of Bolita was a numbers game operated by the Mafia out of Havana, Cuba. The game was very popular in Gulf Hammock with the mill workers—at one point around 600. A large number of workers bought their number(s) during the week, and the winning number was announced on Saturday afternoon. There was much excitement!

In 1959, Fidel Castro led a revolution in Cuba and overthrew the Batista dictatorship. The Mafia immediately left Cuba, thus ending the game of Bolita.

The Author's Comment:

The author only placed a bet once and lost!

Those Were the Times

Chapter 10

Strange Things Actually Do Happen!

Tenth grade has ended and it's the beginnin' of summer, Mr. Gavin asked me if I would fill in at the store until they hired someone full-time. He also told me that he had hired a man named Wild Cat Jones to repair a fifteen foot section of floor in back of the meat case. The job did not pay well at all, and I was not surprised. This was not the first summer I had spent time workin' at the store. Mr. Gavin demands as much work from someone as he can git, cheap as he can git, and the employee must meet high standards.

I think Mr. Gavin is goin' to experience some high frustration in trying to make demands on Wild Cat Jones. For the folk in Greater Gulf Hammock that know him (like him or not), Wild Cat Jones is a free spirit! I know Wild Cat rather well. He lives out on the bank of the Wekiva River in a heavily wooded area with his wife, two young daughters, and two sons. One son is very young and the other son is about my age and is a good friend. (Later on, I will tell you about midnight Wild Cat huntin' trips and story tellin', but for now, back to Wild Cat's first day on the job.)

Wild Cat went to work at about eight o'clock after listenin' to all of Mr. Gavin's expectations. He took a break about ten o'clock, got a "free Pepsi," and went out front by the gas pumps and started a conversation with an older couple that had visited Miami and were goin' back home to New York. Wild Cat could be very entertainin'. He had assumed his humorous country cracker role and was askin' if they had 'wrastled' any alligators.

He had been out front only a few minutes before Mr. Gavin discovered Wild Cat was gone and was out front visitin' customers. It was easy to tell that Mr. Gavin was mad. He interrupted the conversation and told Wild Cat he needed to git back on the job. Wild Cat smiled and told Mr. Gavin that he always took a short mornin' and afternoon break with a "free Pepsi." He then turned his attention back to the tourist and finished his conversation before goin' back to work.

When he went back into the store, Mr. Gavin was waitin'. He told Wild Cat he was to check with him before takin' any more breaks. Wild Cat gave him a smile, then gave him a little salute, and went back to work. I have never seen anyone madder than Mr. Gavin!

Wild Cat Jones kept Mr. Gavin on edge up to the point that he was within two and a half or three days finishin' the job when Wild Cat left on Friday evenin'. He told Mr. Gavin he would finish by the middle of the comin' week.

On the comin' Monday when Wild Cat was to be back at work, he did not show up. Mr. Gavin was gettin' more and more concerned when Jim Clary, the State of Florida Game Warden assigned to Levy County, drove up. He told Mr. Gavin that Wild Cat Jones was in jail over at Bronson, the county seat. It was then that Mr. Gavin exploded! He was becomin' angrier by the minute. Mr. Gavin called Bronson and finally got the judge on the phone. He explained the situation to the county judge and wanted Wild Cat released and returned to Gavin's Store until he finished his job. Then, Wild Cat could be returned to Bronson to serve his time. Judgin' from the look on Mr. Gavin's face, the judge must have told Mr. Gavin he could not do that!

Mr. Gavin was almost shoutin' over the phone at the judge.

"You damn better listen. I went all out to git your ass elected, and I can go all out to git your ass out!"

There was a pause in the phone conversation. The judge must have said he had no way to get Wild Cat to Gavin's Store. Mr. Gavin told the judge to contact Sheriff

G.T. Robbins and have him bring Wild Cat within the hour and then slammed the phone down. Sheriff Robbins was at Gavin's Store within forty-five minutes. Wild Cat was all smiles and finished his work in two days. Sheriff Robbins returned him to Bronson to serve jail time for moonshinin'.

A few weeks later, one of the most unreal things happened. It was one of those things that no one would have believed unless it was in "Ripley's Believe It or Not!"

There was a man and his wife that lived in a wooded area not very far from Wild Cat Jones' family. It seems they had some bad feelings based on something that had just happened. They came in Gavin's Store, and the man had two black eyes and other bruise marks on his head.

The incredible story he shared was that a deputy police officer pulled up in back of their car with patrol lights flashin'. The officer came around to the driver's side of their car, opened the door, and hit him in the head three or four times. Then he went back to his police car and drove around them on toward town. The police officer was none other than Wild Cat Jones—the same Wild Cat Jones who had served time for moonshinin' just six weeks before! At times, I can't help but wonder about the strange things that happen in The Hammock.

On a Monday mornin', Wild Cat Jones' son, Wallace, came to work at Gavin's Store. I was surprised and pleased. I did not realize he had been offered the job, and now I was free for the next week or so before goin' to work at the mill for the rest of the summer. I was asked by Mrs. Gavin to stay the balance of the day and work with Wallace.

A short time later, Wild Cat Jones came by, and he was drivin' a Levy County deputy police car. He was dressed in a fancy deputy police uniform and, as usual, was wearin' his smile. He asked me if I could plan to go wild cat huntin' the comin' Saturday night and that Wallace would pick me up Saturday afternoon. I was interested in goin'.

Providin' a little history, back some years ago, there was a bounty paid on bobcats. We called them "wild cats" in

Gulf Hammock. As I best remember, the bounty was between one and two dollars. You had to bring their right front paw to an office in Bronson to collect the bounty.

I've been told that Wild Cat would cut off all four paws and, over a period of time, try and git paid for all four paws by convincing the folks in Bronson that he could not tell "left from right" nor "front from rear." I was convinced that Wild Cat Jones was one very convincin' person.

Wallace picked me up at home that Saturday afternoon, and we went to meet Wild Cat at their home. The huntin' dogs knew they were goin' huntin', and their barkin' could be heard a quarter of a mile away. They were ready to go! Wild Cat hollered at them to quiet down and they did.

The huntin' car had been adapted to hunt the cats and was not a thing of beauty. It had a large wooden box wedged in a hole in the back for the dogs. It looked like a wreck lookin' for a place to happen, but it was surprisin' how well it could travel in the rugged sand hills and not git stuck. Wallace found where he wanted to start the hunt and parked.

He had told me that his father would release the dogs and start the hunt at exactly twelve o'clock midnight. He said that was the time the wild cats started their hunt for rabbits. It was now ten o'clock in the evenin' and it was time to build a fire and tell stories 'til midnight.

Wild Cat looked over at me and while smilin' said, "Jack, let's hear a story from you."

> "The story I would like to tell is more of a question. It's something I don't understand and maybe it wasn't meant to be understood. I'm sure you have noticed that for each kind of critter in the hammock, that their young look like them—young coons or possums or whatever critters—the young looks like the parents. On the other hand, people seem to have serious differences. As one example, there is a couple that lives down the street from us that is

> one of the ugliest couple I have ever seen. Now here is somethin' strange - they have a really pretty daughter!
>
> You might think that he has a pretty wife! No, he has an ugly wife. She is almost as ugly as he is! Now how can two such ugly people have such a pretty daughter? There is another puzzle. Suppose she had a baby with a handsome young man. Could the baby turn out to be as ugly as her parents or perhaps half again as ugly?"

Wild Cat began laughin'—tryin' to laugh and talk at the same time. He asked, "Does this question have anythin' special to do with you and this pretty young lady?"

"No!" I answered quickly, "But it may be so sometime in the future."

I did not think he and Wallace would stop laughin' long enough to git on to another story.

Wallace and I decided it was Wild Cat's turn to tell a story. Wild Cat agreed and began.

> "It was about five years ago that one of my kin folk came to visit for a few days. He wanted to go cat huntin' the last Saturday night he was here. It was a full moon and a clear night. The dogs sensed we were goin' and about drowned us out with their barkin' and howlin' sounds. They were ready to go! We loaded up and went just north of Wekiva Springs. There were five of us. My cousins and I had stopped by and picked up two of the young Watkins brothers.
>
> We stopped about eleven o'clock and then sat around and told a few stories and decided it was time to hunt. The dogs were more than ready. They struck a fresh cat scent quickly and let out

a loud chorus of barkin'. They had a hot trail and treed the cat in less than a quarter of a mile.

When we reached the scene, the cat was in a scrub oak tree. He was out on a limb not more than twelve feet above the ground. I had my gun ready to shoot the cat.

However, my cousin asked me not to shoot him. He said he would like to climb up and shake the cat out and let the dogs have a fight. I was a little afraid of injuries to the dogs, but the Watkins boys wanted to see the fight too.

My cousin said he would climb up and shake the cat off the limb. I didn't think it was a good idea, but before I could stop him, he was on his way. I knew there was a problem. For one, my cousin was overweight. The second thing was I could not tell if the limb the cat was on was green. Any way, it was too late.

The dogs sensed what was about to happen and there was an increase in loud and now fierce barkin'. It turned out the limb was slightly rotten, and well, with my cousin's weight, was there a problem?...yep, all of a sudden there was a large crackin' sound, and my cousin, the limb, and an angry wild cat crashed to the ground!

I can still remember the loud screechin', anger, and hurt—sounds all blended together.

Finally, the cat broke out of the tangled mess of fightin' critters with my cousin in the mix.

The cat made a dash for higher ground with the dogs frantically barkin' close behind. This could go down as my worst hunt.

First thing I had to do was to find out the damage to my cousin and to be sure he was still alive. From certain hurtful sounds, I guessed that he was. By lookin' him over with a flashlight, I could see he needed some medical care. I hated to take him to Gulf Hammock and wake up that company doctor. He was not gentle. His doctorin' could hurt you at least as much as a wild cat bite or scratch or a dog bite. By the way my cousin was carrying on, he had both dog bites and wild cat bites and scratches.

The Watkins boys checked out my cousin and they agreed he could use a doctor. He hollered the loudest when we covered them bites and scratches with Watkins Liniment.

We then went to git the dogs. They had tracked another cat and were unhappy when we decided to let the cat go, load 'em up and head for the doctor.

I dropped the Watkins boys off, dropped Wallace and the dogs at home, and headed with my cousin to see the doctor. In no way did I want to wake him up!"

The story that Wild Cat told about wakin' the doctor was a horror story! The nurse's son was one of my best friends. I had stopped by his house the next afternoon to find out more about the story of Wild Cat and the doctor. It definitely was a horror story! His mother said the doctor called Wild Cat every name in the "book of profane names," then called her to come to the clinic and doctor up Wild Cat's cousin, then he went back to bed. She was the one who ended up doctorin' Wild Cat's cousin.

I asked her if Wild Cat continued to maintain his "smile" durin' his meetin' with Dr. Kamack. It must have had a terrible impact on Wild Cat as she replied with a laugh, "I heard he briefly lost his smile!"

The last story I will share is extremely difficult to believe! It did happen in the front of the Commissary Store of the Patterson- McInnis Lumber Company. It was pay day and there was a huge crowd. The Commissary Store is a large frame buildin' about fifty feet wide and three hundred feet long. There was a hot rumor that a man from over around Tidewater was comin' to the Commissary to kill Wild Cat Jones and Wild Cat was there! The man's reason for wantin' to kill was—jealousy?

Wild Cat was comin' out of the store when the two saw each other. They approached one another when the man from Tidewater pulled his gun and shot Wild Cat in the chest. They stood facin' each other—I guess they were both waitin' for Wild Cat to fall over dead, but Wild Cat did not fall over dead! The gun misfired and the bullet stuck in Wild Cat's chest creating only a minor injury. Another miracle?

Chapter 11
The Last Days of the Hermits

There was a time, I'm told, that followin' the last days of the Timucuan Indians that the vast region called Greater Gulf Hammock was becomin' populated with inhabitants with vastly different interests. The lumber mills were comin' with an eye on the giant cypress trees along the small rivers, streams, ponds, and in other areas of the low hammock as well as other desirable timber. Thousands of wild cattle were introduced and thrived in the region. The region was becomin' a hunter's paradise.

Much earlier, it had attracted a very different form of wild life. Scattered across this vast area were a "very few" unique individuals called hermits. They preferred to live in isolation; however, times would be changin'.

School is now out after ninth grade for the summer, and I plan to spend some family time, help Joe and Bull Berryhill cut some winter firewood, and spend the balance of time workin' at the mill. Little did I know the kinds of things that would happen before this summer was over.

It all started when I went out to the Berryhills to help Bull and Joe cut firewood. It was about the third day of our cuttin' that Bull stopped and told me and Joe that he saw Joe Glaze, the hermit, comin' up the small dirt road in our direction. The dirt road came past the Berryhill property and ended a short distance away at Highway 19/98.

I had heard of Joe Glaze and that he was a hermit who lived in a homemade shack on the bank of Ten Mile Creek. The shack was located in a remote area of Greater Gulf

Hammock near the Gulf of Mexico. At one point in time, this was a very wild and inaccessible area.

I had never met a hermit. I was shocked at his appearance. His large bony frame was over six feet tall, and he was wearin' an old shapeless cotton broad rimmed hat pulled down to just above his steel gray eyes. He was wearin' a worn out pair of baggy coveralls. The straps of the coveralls hung down to his knees. They reached the top of an old pair of rubber boots. It was difficult to see his face as it was covered by a thick, long stringy beard. He was carryin' an old double barrel twelve gage shotgun.

Joe Glaze just nodded his head toward us and that was the extent of our greetin'. Bull told me he was waitin' on Mrs. Berryhill, and in a few minutes, she appeared carryin' a good size package wrapped in newspapers that she gave to Joe Glaze. He, in turn, gave her a good size package made from woven cabbage fans. They spoke for a few minutes or two, and he walked on to Highway 19/98. He turned north and continued toward Gulf Hammock.

I was curious and wanted to know more about Joe Glaze as well as perhaps more about other hermits. I thought my best source to learn more would be Mr. C.D. Tummond, the Payroll Master for the Patterson-McInnis Lumber Co. in Gulf Hammock.

After two weeks of cuttin' firewood, I thanked Mrs. Berryhill. I only had about ten more days off before goin' back to work at the mill and that would finish off the summer. I said good-bye to everyone and left for home.

I was up early Monday mornin' when I went to the Commissary Store to check if I could see Mr. C.D. Tummond. As I said, he was the Payroll Master—for the largest lumber company in the south.

It was a stroke of good luck. He was fixin' to take a trip to a big loggin' operation in a region of Greater Gulf Hammock called Buck Island. There was a small village there made up of box car houses. Workers and their families would live there until the region was "logged out." There was a school for children, a store, and other needed resources. When this area was "logged out," the "Box Car Village" was moved to another region to be "logged out."

This was a tough life considerin' the hard work, ticks, and lots of other bitin' insects and, at times, bad weather.

Mr. C.D. cranked up the motor rail car, and we were at the Buck Island Box Car Village within a half hour. We left there and travelin' by rail, we crossed over a trestle at Cow Creek and proceeded to Ten Mile Creek. When we crossed over the trestle, we stopped so Mr. C.D. could talk with Joe Glaze, the hermit. He lived in a very small homemade shack with three barkin' dogs tied to the side of the shack. We saw Joe Glaze walkin' up from the bank of Ten Mile Creek toward us. He nodded at me, and Mr. C.D. greeted him. I looked around as Joe Glaze and Mr. C.D. begun to talk.

I learned that Joe Glaze was here before the lumber mills were here. This was a very remote and isolated area of Greater Gulf Hammock at that time. Joe Glaze was the true definition of a hermit. He had withdrawn to a solitary place for a life of peaceful seclusion. He had found what he had searched for. I am not sure how long Joe Glaze was allowed to enjoy his "solitary place." However, I did learn that it was not nearly long enough for him.

First, the hunter's came from nearby towns and cities. They learned that Greater Gulf Hammock was a hunter's paradise. Then came the lumber mills. The first was a crate mill and then came one of the largest mills in the south. This was Groves Dowling Lumber Company. They built the town of Gulf Hammock and went bankrupt in 1926. In 1930 Patterson-McInnis Lumber Company came and "here we are." Joe Glaze is no longer livin' the peaceful seclusion of a hermit in a solitary place.

For another thing, Patterson-McInnis Lumber Co. had leased a rather large tract of land to a company in Cedar Key to cut cabbage tree buds to be used to make brushes, brooms, and other such commodities. This property is not far from Joe Glaze's shack.

People, and people activities, have been closing in on Joe Glaze. At about the same time, a fire burned over one hundred acres of timber land belonging to Patterson-McInnis Lumber Co. It was rumored that Joe Glaze set the fire. To my knowledge, he didn't respond to the rumor. Another rumor was that Joe Glaze hinted that thousands more acres of timber land may burn if anyone tried to force him off his property. He claimed that in the long time past, he had applied for squatter's rights to gain his ownership of the land where his shack is located.

So! This is the main reason that Mr. C.D. came out for a visit with Joe Glaze. He assured Joe that Patterson-McInnis was not tryin' to force him off the land where his shack was located. This wasn't the first time Mr. C.D. had come out to visit Joe Glaze.

When Mr. C.D. and I left Joe Glaze, Mr. C.D. said he was convinced that Joe did believe that it was not Patterson-McInnis Lumber Co. that was trying to force him off his land. Patterson-McInnis owned one hundred thirty-two thousand acres! However, if someone was tryin' to force Joe Glaze off his land, who was it? I became very curious.

I thought my best chance of findin' out was to ask Sheriff G.T. Robbins. I got to know him by playin' against him in the Summer Suwannee Valley Baseball League. He was the catcher for the Bronson town team, and I played for the Gulf Hammock town team. He stopped by Gavin's Store quite often when I worked there. I had a few chances to talk to him and found out quite a lot about Joe Glaze. He had, in the past, been charged two times with attempted murder and found not guilty. Joe Glaze had served a brief period of time in the state prison and been given an early release. The sheriff was not sure why.

I learned that Joe Glaze was charged with firin' a shotgun into an occupied car in 1926 with intent to kill the two occupants in the car. At the end of the trial, the jury found Joe Glaze not guilty. The judge was J.C. Sale.

Then, in 1936, the charges brought against Joe Glaze were the same as the 1926 trial. The only difference was ten years later, a different car and occupants, a different jury, and the same judge, J.C. Sale. The jury found Joe Glaze not guilty. However, the pressure was buildin' to force Joe Glaze out of his shack and out of Greater Gulf Hammock—regardless if he did have squatter's rights!

Followin' the 1936 trial of Joe Glaze, I learned that Judge J.C. Sale contacted the Governor and requested he send someone to Gulf Hammock to investigate Joe Glaze and "his threats to burn timber land belongin' to Patterson-McInnis Lumber Company." There were no direct threats made by Joe Glaze to burn timber land. There were only rumors of a threat, and they were never responded to by Joe Glaze.

It was not long after Judge Sales requested the Governor to send someone to investigate Joe Glaze and threats to burn timber land belongin' to Patterson-McInnis Lumber Company that a terrible event happened. Joe Glaze's small shack was soaked in gasoline and burned while he was away. His three dogs were tied to the shack at the time of the fire! They also burned.

I learned of this not too long after it happened—about two days. I was drivin' south on Highway 19/98 in my brother's car and saw someone walkin' south beyond where Ten Mile Creek crosses Highway 19/98. I was shocked because it was Joe Glaze.

I pulled off the side of the road and tried to speak, but he ignored me and continued to walk south. He stopped a short distance away and started slowly walkin' back toward me. I waited. He walked up close to me and held out his hand. I held his hand for a moment. He turned and slowly continued his walk south. I never heard of Joe Glaze again, but I thought of him often. I hoped he could find some secluded place where he could live in isolation and peace for the balance of his life. There was no such place left in Greater Gulf Hammock where a hermit could live a solitary and peaceful life.

The hermits suffered the same fate as had the Indians. They were forced out. Other bad news was on the horizon.

Patterson-McInnis Lumber Mill was closin'. The mill was up for sale—includin' all houses and other buildin's. Houses and other buildin's must be moved from the mill property within a specified deadline. This decision created an incredible emotional and financial hardship on workers who worked for low pay and had no savings. Most had school age children.

The mill was sold to a large corporation for scrap metal, and in the early salvage process, the mill caught on fire. It was the largest fire ever in the experience of the entire county. The mill burned in 1957. The lumber mill fire ended the era of the lumber mills in Gulf Hammock.

My father died in 1958. He had spent almost all of his workin' life in Greater Gulf Hammock and chose to be buried there rather than be returned to South Alabama where all of his Foley relatives were buried. Greater Gulf Hammock was his home! Greater Gulf Hammock was sold to a large international paper corporation.

Now the Indians, the hermits, the wandering gypsies, and the lumber mills are all gone, and Greater Gulf Hammock has become a large corporate tree farm with lots of fences.

The Author's Historic Note

The Atlantic Coastline Railroad was completed through Gulf Hammock around 1913. The railroad included an excellent station. There were many packages shipped to and from Gulf Hammock as well as some passengers using the train. The train station was a great asset to the town of Gulf Hammock. The Atlantic Coastline Railroad continued to operate until 1967 but after the mid-fifties, no longer stopped in Gulf Hammock.

The Author's Comment:

The end of the mill was the end of the town.

Chapter 12

A Short Story—Believe It or Not, It's True!

Two brothers own a small, portable lumber mill that sits on about 50 heavily wooded acres located north of Gulf Hammock. The brothers not only harvest lumber for sale from their property, but they also contract to harvest lumber from other property owners.

The brothers are married to two sisters. One of the brothers begins to notice that his brother's wife looks more attractive than his wife. When they married, each brother built their wife a house not far from the mill so the families saw each other on a regular basis.

The brother who was becoming more and more attracted to his brother's wife decided he would discuss this with his brother. He was very much afraid that his brother would get upset and there would be big trouble. The brother decided to take a chance as his brother had always admired his horse and loved money. He decided he would offer to trade his horse, wife, and forty dollars in exchange for his brother's wife. The trade was made.

However, when the two wives found out about their husband's deal, there were fireworks, two mad sisters, and two divorces!

If you are ever over in the area described above, there are two unemployed men and two attractive "well to do" ladies!

Those Were the Times

Chapter 13

The Company Doctor

To the best of my knowledge, Doctor Gavin was one of the first doctors who served the saw mill workers and their families in Gulf Hammock. He also served other individuals in the region who were in need.

Doctor Lafayette came after Doctor Gavin, and I remember him well. He had a large wooden barrel sitting just outside his clinic. The barrel contained live rattle snakes. The rattle snakes provided him with a source of venom as he was in contact with someone from south Florida who was doin' research with the venom. There were also other stories of his use of the snakes...

Then came Dr. Kamack! For injured males, he was the most feared person in the Gulf Hammock region! Dr. Kamack was known to be rough in his treatment of injured males—both men and boys! I can attest to rough treatment on two different occasions as I had first-hand experiences.

The first experience happened while I was using a grass sling. The grass sling hit a rock and came over on top of my left bare foot. I was cut across the entire top of my foot. I ran all the way to the doctor's office which was not too far away. The nurse showed a great deal of concern but not Dr. Kamack! He did not show any concern and was in no hurry. The nurse quickly washed the dirt and blood away from the cut.

Dr. Kamack did not use anything to deaden the pain. He simply poured alcohol on the cut which burned like fire. Then he began to sew up the cut by using a large needle and some type of heavy thread. It was very painful, and he showed no concern.

I told him this was the last time I would come to him for any doctorin', and he called me a "damn baby."

Unfortunately, the first day that school was out the followin' summer, I stepped on a nail that was stickin' up through a board. It was in heavy grass, and the nail was not visible. As much as I hated it, I had to go back to Dr. Kamack. I had to eat crow before he would do one thing. The nurse encouraged me to eat crow quickly—and I did!

On another occasion, my younger brother, Don, needed to see the doctor. He refused to go to the office with mother. She tried her best to encourage him to go, but he still refused! Mother walked to the clinic and met with Dr. Kamack. He was always considerate with females, and he offered to give her a ride home in his car and he would see Don there. Don saw them coming and tried to hide. However, he was not quick enough and the chase was on. I was home and could enjoy watching the chase! It was much like seeing someone chase a wild chicken. At one point, Don almost got away. However, they hemmed him up in the far corner of the back yard. He had no choice, with mother there, but to be examined by Dr. Kamack.

I never really knew what was wrong with Don nor anything about the cure, but after being run down by mother and Dr. Kamack, Don recovered very quickly!

Dr. Kamack was with Patterson-McInnis Lumber Company the entire length of their stay in Greater Gulf Hammock. For many years, Dr. Kamack delivered babies for women who needed his assistance in all towns in Levy County and some towns beyond. He was highly regarded by the women including my mother—he delivered my two youngest sisters, Faye and Janice. His charge was $25 for delivery and initial care if needed and $35 for a delivery and any initial care beyond Levy County.

Stories by Jack Foley

The Author's Historic Note

The Groves Dowling Lumber Company, including all holdings, filed for bankruptcy in 1929. All Grove Dowling properties and holdings were auctioned off at the Levy County Courthouse in Bronson, Florida, in 1930 and were purchased by Patterson-McInnis Lumber Company (under the name of Robinson Land and Lumber Company). The bid price was $1 million.

The Author's Comment:

This 1930 transaction saved the town of Gulf Hammock. The new lumber mill was to become the largest in the "South!"

Chapter 14

Excitement at Cedar Key!

One thing I quickly learned was that students from Bronson were well known by all teachers and teachers also knew their parents. However, the vast majority of neither teachers nor administrators knew the parents of "bussed in" students. We had already been told that students from Bronson were often treated a little more special than those who were "bussed in." I learned the first day of school there was some truth to that information and later that there were certain teachers who were exceptions to the rule.

When we arrived at school the first mornin', there was someone at the bus stop who directed all ninth graders to follow them to their home room. There we were directed to find a vacant seat and be seated where we would soon receive our directions for the day.

I looked around for a vacant seat. There was one I spotted at the end of a back row. I also noticed that there was a very attractive girl with blond hair seated next to the last seat in that row. She turned and looked back at me, sportin' a big smile and introduced herself. Before I could introduce myself, a boy came up to my desk and rudely told me to move—that this was "his seat."

I told him in no uncertain terms that I would not move and if I did, it would be toward him. Before the situation became worse, the homeroom teacher came up and without lookin' at me, she asked the student, by name, and in a friendly manner "what was the problem?"

He told her that I was in his seat. Before I could explain, she asked me to find another seat. I told her no and asked her to let me explain. She said no, and again asked me to move.

Again, I told her no, and she said move or she would send me to the principal. I told her fine, and she promptly wrote a note and asked me to leave and carry it to the principal's office. I told her I did not know where the principal's office was located. She then asked the attractive girl with blond hair to escort me to the principal's office. I got to know her a little better on the way to the office!

After reading the note from the homeroom teacher, the principal asked me to go ahead and attend my classes and come back to his office after school. I told the principal that I could not go to classes as I didn't know what classes to attend nor where the classes were held.

After the last class, I had to catch the school bus back to Gulf Hammock. The principal seemed tired already, and it was just the first day of school! He walked me back to the homeroom, got my schedule, and then showed me my classes and my classrooms. Lo and behold, my first class was Algebra I, and he was my teacher!

There are times when good things happen that can outweigh unpleasant happenings. It did happen that the ninth grade school would end on a good note! The last bus trip home at the end of ninth grade was really loud. It became somewhat quieter when Mrs. Mozo let off the Otter Creek students. She then let the Gulf Hammock students off in front of the Gulf Hammock school house.

I had been deep in thought of how the ninth grade school year had started and how it had ended. As I started walkin' home, my thoughts were interrupted from sounds comin' from the area of Hands Swimmin' Hole.

It's located a short distance through the woods at a creek that flows through a heavily wooded area. This swimmin' hole is a "boys only swimmin' hole" as they swim naked, and girls are not allowed.

However, some girls have been known to sneak in and steal the boys' clothes and leave them out in the street for the world to see! The boys always pick the smallest or most vulnerable boys to run out and grab the clothes and bring them back.

I made my way through the thick, wooded area to the creek bank and saw two boys chasin' and splashin' water on each other. They both were excellent swimmers and did not see me for a brief period of time. When they did, one of them hollered "who the hell are you?"

I hollered back, "who the hell are the two of you?" They started swimmin' back in my direction. When they arrived at the bank of the creek below where I was standin', it was Horace who told me their names were Horace and Nathan Fine.

Horace did most all the talkin'. He said their stepfather had taken a job at the lumber mill. Nathan said he and Horace had only been in Gulf Hammock two days and they already hated the place and planned to go back to Cedar Key soon with or without the rest of the family.

I told them that my father, brothers, and I would go with friends to Cedar Key in the winter when red fish were comin' in. We fished at the Number 4 Bridge. I also told them I played baseball on the Gulf Hammock town team, and we played the Cedar Key town team.

It turned out that some of the players I knew on the Cedar Key town team were related to Horace and Nathan. Their entire family was unhappy livin' in Gulf Hammock, and they decided, after a brief period of time, to all go back to Cedar Key.

Horace and Nathan asked me if I would come to Cedar Key and do some fishin' with them. They said we could each make more money than I could make at the lumber mill. It sounded much more excitin' than workin' as a stick boy in the lumber yard at the mill.

I told them I had no place to stay in Cedar Key, and they said their family had arranged to move into an old, large frame house close to the Number 4 Bridge. If I wanted, I could stay there with them as they had an extra cot in their room.

Mother was not happy and was against the idea. My father left the decision up to me. I told Horace and Nathan to ask their step-father and mother about me comin' to Cedar Key and stayin' with them to do some fishin'.

After all agreements were made, I told Horace and Nathan that I needed time to work with my father cuttin' some wood for the winter which would need time to dry out. I would come down to join them in Cedar Key in about eight or nine days and that I would have no problem catchin' a ride. I knew the mill had a loggin' crew in that region and they had a log truck haulin' to the mill in Gulf Hammock every day.

In eight days, I caught a ride on a log truck! The driver of the truck was Bug Watkins, and I was friends with their family. Bug reminded me of a story my older brother, Fred, had told about Cedar Key. He said they did not like "outsiders" there and especially after dark. This was especially so of the younger Cedar Key men and boys.

The story is told that one night, some young men from Cedar Key caught my brother, Fred, and three of his friends after dark on a Saturday night. To make matters worse, they had dates with some Cedar Key girls. Far outnumbered, Fred and his friends were blocked and forced out of their car.

They were escorted to the Number 4 Bridge goin' out of Cedar Key, and their car was driven across the Number 4 Bridge leavin' them on the opposite side. They were given the keys to their car and told that "the next time they would have to wade through the Channel to reach their car and go home."

They also told Fred and his friends things would be much worse the next time they were caught after dark in Cedar Key. It had been several years before that I had heard about this supposingly happenin'. I made a note to ask Horace and Nathan about this story.

Bug drove past where he was supposed to turn off and go to the loggin' area and took me on to the Number 4

Bridge. I thanked Bug and walked over to the rather large, old weather beaten house where I was greeted by Horace and Nathan's mother and was told where I could find them.

They were workin' on a net and a boat not far from the Number 4 Bridge. I caught up with them there and told them about the trip with Bug and the story my brother had told about his experience in Cedar Key. They did not seem surprised and told me not to be concerned and to just tell anyone that asks that I am stayin' with Horace and Nathan.

We spent some time workin' on the boat and visitin'. That night, we all went to bed early. The next day was Saturday, and Horace and Nathan had been invited to go on a fishin' trip with some friends. I was invited, but declined as I wanted to enjoy a peaceful day at the dock and maybe do some fishin'.

Then, I planned to visit with Dallas Booth who operated the Little Skipper Restaurant which was located on the dock.

Dallas played third base for the Cedar Key baseball town team, and I played first base for the Gulf Hammock town team. The two teams played each other two games durin' the summer season, and that's how we got to know each other.

My plans for the day were workin' out great, but went downhill fast! I had a hamburger at the Little Skipper and visited with Dallas Booth. I was leavin' the Little Skipper and was stopped by three boys about my age.

One of the boys, who did all of the talkin' asked me who I was and what was I doin' in Cedar Key. I told him that I was stayin' with Horace and Nathan Fine and planned on stayin' to do some fishin' for a while.

He told me that I was not stayin' in Cedar Key and gave me one day to be gone or else! I did not want to end up in a fight there and certainly not three against one. I told the one that was doin' all the talkin' that I would give my friends his message. He interrupted me and said leave by dark and my friends will find out plenty soon.

Thanks to good timin', Horace and Nathan got back early, and the family had already planned a fish fry at their kin folks' home. I told them of the incident at the dock and was surprised they did not seem very concerned! Their stepfather said he would take care of it and in the meantime, I was to stick with him or Horace.

Horace said it was about time to go over to their grandma's house, and we would have a little time to visit before the fish would be ready. I was not ready for the shock! When we walked into the front yard, the first people we saw were the three boys that had stopped me at the dock and ordered me out of Cedar Key! Nathan spoke first.

"Cooper," he said. "He told you he was visitin' with us and he will only leave if or when we say so."

The argument was headin' in the direction of a fight when Dallas Booth came around the corner along with (who I learned later) was another brother named Wesley Booth. I also learned later that the Booth family was closely related to the Fine family. Cooper was caught in an embarrassing situation and was forced to back down.

A few days later, I went by the Little Skipper's for a hamburger and found Cooper there. He was seated with Dallas who was not busy at the time. Dallas waved me over to sit with them. I could tell that Dallas and maybe Wesley had talked with Cooper. He was a little friendlier, and over time, we became friends.

We finally got the fishin' boat and nets ready for fishin'. The boat was about 18' long with the inside walk boards about 14" wide running from bow to stern on the port and starboard side. By using the push pole and walkin' the walk board, you could push the boat. The speed and direction of the board depends on your strength and how well you can use a push pole and walk a walk board. Only a few fishermen had an outboard motor which gave them a significant advantage over the "walk board" boats.

On our very first fishin' trip, I made a bad mistake. Nathan spotted a school of mullet, and we moved in that direction. As we got close, Nathan called to me to drop the weight tied to the lead line of the net.

I dropped the wrong lead line which pulled the entire net overboard! I won't repeat all the bad things that came spewin' out of Nathan's mouth. It took some extra time and work, but we finally made a good strike.

My mistake never seemed to bother Horace. He included it in with his many humorous stories. Nathan never seemed to think it was humorous however.

Another story that Horace told with humor was that on one fishin' trip, he and Nathan made a real good strike and had a lot of mullet trapped in the center of a net laid out in a circular shape. They were wading in the center of the circular net and beatin' on the top of the water with short wooden poles to run the mullet into the net.

By accident, Nathan stepped on a stingray and got hit just above the ankle. This is an extremely painful injury. Horace quickly made sure that Nathan was safely in the boat and started to quickly pole the boat back to the Cedar Key dock to get Nathan to the doctor. Horace knew that Nathan was in great pain. He decided to try and entertain Nathan to get some of this attention off the pain.

"Nathan," Horace shouted. "Watch this spectacular event! I'm going to push this old boat as fast as I can and get enough speed that I can turn a back flip over the back of the boat, grab the stern, flip back in the boat, grab the push pole, and keep speedin' for the dock."

He did get attention from Nathan, and Horace did attempt the back flip, but unfortunately, he came back down on the stern of the boat. His back was injured severely enough that he could no longer pole the boat.

Nathan was forced, with severe pain, to pole the boat to the dock and take himself and Horace to the doctor. This became one more story that Horace fixed up and added to his collection of humorous stories—but it was never humorous to Nathan!

Those Were the Times

One of Horace's and Nathan's good friends, Mo Beckham, said if you ever saw a crowd of people really laughin' in Cedar Key, you could bet they were gathered around Horace Fine and that he was engaged in humorous story tellin'! He was a great storyteller!

Horace and I planned to fish near Sea Horse Key late one Saturday afternoon. It was a full moon, and he told me that after the full moon is up, we may see "ghosts" at Sea Horse Key.

Horace says the ghosts may include a headless horseman who rides on nights of the full moon or a white mule may appear as the ghost of a fair young maiden who was killed by her evil lover. Horace even said you can also hear voices of men talkin' when no one is there as well as other ghostly entities.

I was not sure I wanted to become involved with a collection of ghosts. However, if they were recommended by Horace, I'd stay and witness the ghost show. We waited for more than three hours and no ghosts. However, a large school of mullet showed up. It was the largest strike we had made since I had been fishin' with Horace.

During the followin' weeks, Horace and I did some hook and line fishin' from the dock. The red fish were comin' in with the tides and Horace was in a story tellin' mood. I was curious about things I had heard about Cedar Key. One thing was their attitude toward "outsiders." Horace said, "For young boys," it seemed that it boiled down to saving all Cedar Key girls for Cedar Key boys and to have the excitement of fightin' outsiders rather than each other. For Cedar Key men, it was a "mixed bag." The fishermen lived off the resources provided by the island Gulf waters and they had learned as "boys" to keep out "outsider" males.

I told Horace about Cedar Key families who had moved to Gulf Hammock and the men worked at the mill. They contended that you had to be "born in Cedar Key" to be accepted as bein' from Cedar Key.

Stories by Jack Foley

I had even heard about some stories of Greek sponge fishermen being murdered at Cedar Key. The story ran in "The Levy County Journal" newspaper about 15 years before. Horace did confirm that if you were not born in Cedar Key, then you were not "from Cedar Key" and that you were from someplace else and moved to Cedar Key.

About the Greek sponge fishermen…there was a small settlement of Greeks who had moved to Cedar Key. Some of them had opened a small business or two. Some did sponge fishing and their home location was Tarpon Springs, Florida.

According to the story that was published in the paper, there were three Greek sponge fisherman robbed and killed. Their bodies were placed in the jail, and the jail was then burned. The Cedar Key Justice of Peace and the Cedar Key Special Constable were charged with murder.

Horace and I spent the entire day at the dock and had a good catch fishin'. We kept enough fish for a fish fry and sold the rest. After the fish fry, I planned to talk to Horace and Nathan about me returnin' to Gulf Hammock within the next two or three days but I wanted to have one more day of fishin' from the dock. Even though the summer was only half gone, I started to miss my family, friends, and Gulf Hammock.

I thanked everyone and the next mornin' Horace and I went to the dock. Good luck was with us as we caught and sold a good catch of red fish, and the luck continued. There was a man and his son fishin' at the dock from Dixie County. They were leavin' in a couple of hours and were willin' to drop me off in Otter Creek—only five miles from my home. When I got off in Otter Creek, my luck was still holdin'. Bug Watkins came by in a log truck, and I was home in less than 15 minutes!

Those Were the Times

The Author's Historic Note

June 7, 1927—Mr. J. B. Adkins met with the School Board members and requested the Board build a new school in Gulf Hammock. The School Board could not pay the $25,000 requested. The School Board requested that Mr. Adkins ask Grove Dowling Lumber Company to build the school and the School Board would circulate a bond to reimburse Groves Dowling. This may be the old, empty, and dilapidated church/school building still standing in Gulf Hammock.

The Author's Comment:

"The Gulf Hammock kids deserve a good school." They are smarter and more attractive than those from other towns that are bussed to Bronson and even those from Bronson!

Chapter 15
The Long Hot Days

Kenneth Smallwood and I became friends in the fifth grade at the Gulf Hammock School. He told me of some of the community activities they had almost every year at their farm and invited me to come. Kenneth also asked me if I would like to come early and help them prepare for these activities.

With permission from Mother and Dad, I agreed if it was okay with his parents. Kenneth's parents said it was okay with them if I wanted to come and help, and he said it would involve me stayin' part of the time with his family.

The first activity was a peanut boilin', and the second activity was about three weeks later—cane grindin' and syrup makin'. Lots of people from Gulf Hammock came to both activities, and I enjoyed workin' at both of these community events.

Mr. Smallwood asked me if I would like some summer work when school was out. He said he would pay in produce or maybe ten cents per day for part of the time and in produce for the other part. Mother liked the produce idea!

I learned that life on a farm is a lot of hard work and involves long hours. You are up and workin' before daylight and the day does not stop until the evenin' hours. It is at daylight that all the animals, includin' chickens, have to be fed to get ready for the day. I also learned how to plow a single horse plow as well as a two horse turnin' plow.

After dark was the time to eat supper and what a treat! Mrs. Smallwood was a great cook—like my mother. She also worked in the field plus worked at other necessary chores to help keep the farm runnin'.

Mrs. Smallwood also looked after eight children rangin' in ages from toddler to high school. I was dead tired after supper and went directly to bed after first washin' with water from a hand pump.

Every Sunday, after all mornin' chores were done, we were free! We headed for the Wekiva Swimmin' Hole. Wekiva Springs is located in the sand hills about two miles above the farm and formed the river that ran close to the farm. All of us loved Sundays!

Durin' the summer, I got to know part of the Watkins family who lived near the Smallwoods. They were always at the Wekiva Swimmin' Hole on Sunday afternoons. I learned from them that they had two large mulberry trees in front of their house, and they were loaded with sweet mulberries. I planned to go by there one Sunday afternoon after swimmin'.

The followin' Sunday, instead of goin' directly to the swimmin' hole, I decided to go by the Watkins' place first and check out the mulberries. This ended up bein' more than I expected. The Watkins had a rather large farm with a rather large two-story frame house. They had ten children—all of them older than me, and some were married.

When I came to their gate, I went in and walked down the lane to the front of their house. I noticed an old man sittin' in a rockin' chair, and I shouted, "Hello!"

He shouted back, "Who the hell are you?" and "What the hell do you want?"

I asked him if I might have some mulberries. I told him my name and that I was workin' part of the summer for Mr. Smallwood. He said he would think about me havin' some mulberries and that I was to come back the next Sunday. I thanked him and started to leave.

He stopped me and said he had already changed his mind and that I could go ahead and climb one of the trees but to try not to stand directly below where the birds are concentrated. They had been eatin' lots of mulberries and the mulberries act as a laxative. The man told me I'd get splattered real good!

The old man said "If you are not already a little shithead, you will be!"

I thanked the old man for the mulberries and headed for the swimmin' hole.

I learned from some of "Uncle Jack's" grandchildren the he did have a temper even before he went blind. He had a string that he had tied on one end above the porch door that reached out about 50 feet to the outhouse so he could find his way there and back. He would run his hand along the string and it would guide him. As a joke, someone moved the end from the outhouse and tied it to the hen house.

The end result was not planned! The hens were guarded by a "bad" rooster. This rooster attacked Uncle Jack, and he hollered for help. He said he would find out and beat who did this to an old, blind man. Someone was very lucky that he never found out!

I ended my work on the farm about half way through the summer. Mother loved all the produce and Mr. Smallwood included a very young pig!

When it was all said and done, mother said the pay in "produce from the farm" was well worth the time spent. All I could think was that I didn't get paid a dern thing!

The Author's Historic Note

In 1926, an election was held at Gunntown (the name for Gulf Hammock between 1916 and 1926) to select a paid road-and-bridge district trustee for a period of three years. He would be responsible for overseeing the maintenance of all roads and bridges. LP Smallwood was selected as the trustee. He owned the largest farm in Gulf Hammock.

The Author's Comment:

Mr. Smallwood did have a built-in advantage with a large number of family members and distant kin. He also sponsored annual cane grindings and other popular activities for the community. The author worked on the Smallwood Farm for most of one summer for ten cents per day and board. The author ended up with "no money" but being paid exclusively with farm produce. Only the author's mother was happy with the arrangement.

Chapter 16

The Dreaded Wash Day for Clothes

About every eight days, mother warned my sister, Betty and me, that we will be helpin' her wash clothes startin' in two days, and there will be no excuses! If either of us complains, she will send us both outside to pick out a switch and bring it back so she can give us a good switchin'!

Betty has, on occasion, actually gone out and brought her a switch "such as it was!" She was always very sensitive and quick to tears. I, on the other hand, would always go out but never bring back a switch for I knew if I stayed out long enough, mother would forget.

Mother had so many things to do every day, and I knew she needed to prepare somethin' for dad—like a quick lunch on his work day that by the time Betty came back with a pitiful lookin' excuse for a switch, Mother had forgotten!

The process of washin' and dryin' clothes was far from simple. First, you needed at least three number three wash tubs of "appropriate water" plus extra water for the iron wash pot. The water supplied by the mill was sulfur water and had a terrible smell and also contained iron. If you turned on a faucet, you not only got a bad smell, but the iron content of the water stained everything with an iron cast color.

A week or so before "wash day," mother would set the wash tubs under the eaves of the house to catch the rain water. If luck wasn't with us for rain, we had to carry the water in a five gallon bucket from a small creek that flowed in back of the house and fill up all available tubs and the large iron pot about three quarters full. The iron pot was used to boil some of Dad's clothes in order to get them clean.

The small creek that ran in back of the house was coming from one of the creeks that branched off the Wekiva River. The creeks that branched off the river boasted beautiful, crystal clear water. However, it took time to carry enough buckets of water to fill up these number three wash tubs with enough water needed to complete a washin'. Usually, fillin' the tubs three quarters is enough to get the job done!

All of my father's mill clothes had to be boiled, then beat with a large paddle on a "battling-block"—a circular oak block about 3' tall and 30" in diameter—before goin' through three rinsins'. Paddlin' the clothes on the block helped break loose the tough dirt.

All other clothes, besides my overalls or Levi's, were scrubbed on a scrub board with soapy water and everythin' went through three rinsins'. Everythin' was then hung on a clothes line to dry. By the time this was all done, almost the entire day was gone.

Lookin' back over the day, I'd have to say my sister and I had a good day. On one wash day, I chose a wet pair of our father's long handle underwear and wrapped it around Betty's head. I will never live it down!

The worst thing that ever happened after a wash day was we had hung all the clothes out to dry on the clothes line leavin' enough daylight left to do some huntin'. I went inside the house, got me a rifle, and walked outside decidin' to take a practice shot. I thought one of the clothes pins on the clothes line would be a good target.

What a terrible mistake! I not only hit the clothes pin, but also cut the clothes line, and all the wet clothes came down in the dirt! With Betty's help, we spent 'til after dark repairing the clothes line, carryin' water and havin' to rinse all the clothes again! Betty and I still talk about wash days and the many other good times we had growin' up in the hammock.

We also talk about Mother and what a hard life she lived in Gulf Hammock as well as many other women who were married to mill workers. We both agree that Gulf Hammock did not offer much to women or young girls. In her senior year, Betty moved to Avon Park, Florida, and lived with our aunt and cousins and finished school. I thought she made a good choice—so did Mother even though she missed Betty terribly.

Those Were the Times

Chapter 17

The Last Chapter

I have often thought about certain incidents that occurred with my family and are embedded in my mind. My father and I would often go over to the Waccasassa River early on Sunday and catch enough fish for three or four fish fries. When we caught more than we needed, we always shared with friends.

One Sunday mornin', we were walkin' through the woods toward the Waccasassa and he stopped just before reachin' the river. He walked over to an old, dead log and sat down. I asked him what was wrong, and he told me he needed to think for a few minutes. I became very concerned. In about ten minutes, he said it was wrong for him to fish on Sunday and that he should be in church. We only had one rod and reel and it was his. He asked if I thought it was wrong for me. I told him I would have to think about it, too, but while I was thinkin' about it, I wanted to borrow his rod and reel while I was thinkin' and fishin'. He smiled, handed me the rod and reel and told me to keep thinkin'.

Dad would often surprise me—or maybe impress me would be a better expression. He built all of our furniture except the old iron stove, workin' with his woodwork tools. He made a large wooden tool box and kept it secure with a large lock. It was a very good idea. With me and two other brothers around, it could result in losin' all his tools!

On one occasion, I was helpin' him build a couple of outside benches. He sent me to get one of his tools from his tool box and to hurry along. I started on a fast trot toward the tool box. As I was close to the tool box, I remembered I had not asked him for his key. I had a feelin' Dad had tricked me as I had learned to open his tool box without a key long ago. I was very careful to put the tool I used back in its exact spot and lock the tool box when I was through. I didn't dare carry the tool he wanted back to him so I trotted back and told him he forgot to give me the key.

Dad smiled, reached out and put his hand on my shoulder and said, "I have been very proud of you for quite a while! You always carefully put back every tool that you have taken from my tool box without a key!" I was shocked! He used the tool, handed it back to me, and told me to return it to the tool box. He did not give me a key. With this experience and others, I came to learn that my father was a very wise person.

There was yet another time when my father surprised me. I was comin' home from the Commissary Store and had discovered the Lumber Company was sponsorin' a "turkey shoot" contest. A target was set up and two shots were allowed for each participant. The best of the two shots were counted. The cost was fifty cents for the two shots. A shotgun was provided by Mr. Pettaway, the manager of the mill. He was in charge of the contest. You could use your own shotgun if it was the same caliber.

Dad was tellin' Mr. Pettaway that he did not want two shots. He only needed one and should pay only a quarter. Finally, Mr. Pettaway agreed and Dad sent me home to bring back his shotgun and one shell. Dad won the turkey! He was an outstandin' marksman.

Fredrick was the first born child in our family and from day one he was the favorite with Dad. When "Fred" was very young, maybe seven years old, Dad bought him a five dollar, 22 caliber rifle. He taught him how to use it and began carryin' him huntin'. Fred served with General Patton durin' World War II, and we worried 'til the end of the war, especially Dad. My younger brother, Don, and I would sometimes talk about the strong tie that Dad had with Fred and agreed that it did not affect our love for Dad.

Speakin' of Don, he was six years younger than me, but we did have a good relationship. He was the "marble shark" durin' the marble playin' age at the elementary school. He played for "keeps!" At the latter part of his marble playin' he had a box containin' a large collection of marbles. Don decided he would bury them in a secret place in the edge of the woods close to our house. To the best of my knowledge (and Don's), they are still there but he can't find them!

Money was "very" scarce to workers in Gulf Hammock. I was often thinkin' of some honest way to make some. It occurred to me that there are lots of snakes in Gulf Hammock and I could skin some out and make belts. Don wanted to go with me on my very first snake hunt. We did not have to go far into the woods before I spotted a good size Cottonmouth. It was not in the best area to confront a poisonous snake of his size. Don was in a high, dry area with a full view of the snake. I looked around and found a young tree about seven feet tall that appeared to have recently died. I broke it off—even with the muddy ground. It seemed solid, and I could easily kill the snake with it.

Things did not work well. The area where the snake was located became more and more boggy. I moved slowly and was in range of killin' the snake. He had not moved. I smashed the snake with the pole and discovered the pole was not solid. It was rotten and did not, in any way, hurt the snake. I tried to run but it was too boggy. I fell in the mud on my way out to high ground. Don was rollin' over with laughter! I could find no humor in the situation. I never knew which way the snake went but I do know that I never took Don along again.

I continued my efforts to hunt, kill, and skin snakes. I began to mount the skins on the side of the house, close to Mother's wash house. At this point in time, Mom now had a wash house (made by Dad) with a washin' machine! She demanded the snake skins be removed from "her house" and from "her sight." That was the end of my "snake belt" money makin' plan.

I had noticed early on that I was the only one of the children that Dad called by their given names. He called Fred "Boy," Doris "Nell," Don "Dan," Betty "Joy," Faye "Annie," and Janice "Baby Monkey." Janice hated her name! Mother said my name was legally "Jackie" and it was written in the family Bible.

My father was never a person to argue with anyone. Privately, he told me my name was Jack and that I was the only child he named. Down the road, when I got ready to retire, I had to get a birth certificate. Guess what? My name was Jack—not Jackie! Mom was shocked and could not understand. Well, it so happened that the doctor had asked Dad my name when he was fillin' out the birth certificate. Dad had never shared that information but always called me Jack and used his preferred name for each of the other children.

I never knew my sister Doris very well. She was three years older and ran away from home at around 13 or 14 years old. Doris married what became the meanest man in the region. It was a very difficult marriage, and for many of his criminal acts, he was finally sentenced to prison. She remained close to Mother and would bring her romance paperback novels. Mother loved to read those novels and placed them under her mattress which created a large lump.

My sister, Betty, and I became close as we got into our teenage years. There was a large square dance held on Saturday nights in the town of Inglis. We would sometimes join up with friends and go to the square dance.

On an occasional Saturday afternoon after supper, about 6:00 p.m., some of Dad's friends would gather on our front porch and take turns story tellin'. Kids were not allowed. However, I could come up and sit on the very edge of the porch by the chimney and not be easily seen. I loved to listen as they took turns tellin' stories. No one dared laugh at a serious story, and all joined in laughter at a humorous one. One time, Dad was tellin' a serious story, and one of the listeners made an inappropriate, humorous comment. Dad sent everyone home! To my knowledge, that never did occur again!

This is my senior year in high school! I was already more than a year older than most high school seniors and am beginnin' to get serious about what I'm goin' to do when I graduate. I am surely not goin' to be a "stick boy" at the mill forever. I need to begin to plan!

I did find out that I had to register for the military draft—which the postmaster told me I must do—so I did. I decided I had better become better informed, too. My dad subscribed to the Sunday *St. Petersburg Times* newspaper, and I started to read more than the comics!

I was out of high school for almost a year when a big life changin' event happened. I stopped by the post office and started to open our post office box when the postmaster, Mr. Yearty, called to me and said "Don't open the box." He said my draft notice was in the box and that he would have to inform the draft board that I had picked up the draft notice and signed for it. He said he would hold the notice for several days to give me time to decide what to do.

I received some good advice durin' the next few days—the best from my older brother, Fred. He was an experienced Army combat veteran havin' served durin' World War II. I took his advice and joined the Navy the followin' week. I went through boot camp in San Diego, California. I was then assigned to duty aboard a war ship. The assignment was to the gunnery division on the U.S. Toledo. The ship was bein' prepared to engage in the war in Korea. I had no idea where Korea was. The flashback at the beginnin' of my story picks up from here.

The Author's Historic Note

It has been an enjoyable pleasure to provide you with a journey from the cotton fields of South Alabama to the town of Gulf Hammock and the region of Greater Gulf Hammock.

Those Were the Times

Your journey began durin' the time of a great depression. Even in depression times, there was always food in Greater Gulf Hammock which served up a variety. There was game of all sorts and plenty of fresh and salt water food sources. Many people planted large gardens every spring with lots of sharin' goin' on with the needy. I should simply say that no one went hungry. I do believe that the town and region was harder on girls and women than it was on males! Other than a 10 cent movie once a week in a warehouse, entertainment was very limited—"Not Gene Autry Again!"

I will have to say that during my last year in Gulf Hammock, my range of good times expanded. I bought a car! It was the first car in our family—an old Ford station wagon, not a beauty spot, but it did run good. Just before leavin' home, I went by the courthouse and put the car in my father's name. It was his "first car" and he was very proud of it! Very few of the mill workers owned a car. I did notice that some of my father's friends were gatherin' 'round on a regular basis assistin' my father work on his "new" car and followin' my father's directions as none had ever owned a car!

About the Author

Following the Korean War, Jack Foley attended the University of Florida, receiving his Doctorate with a major in mathematics. He accepted an assistant teaching position for updating teachers at off-campus locations on the "New Mathematics." Among the center locations were Jacksonville, Orlando, and Tampa which provided Dr. Foley the opportunity to network with administrators and educators from rural and urban communities. Through these training sessions, Dr. Foley discovered the greatest concern among the attendees was the number of students who were borderline failures, discipline problems, and potential dropouts. Many of these students were also problems in their communities.

In the 1960's, the United States was ripe for innovation. National support and leadership for educational advancement was readily available, opening doors for constructive improvement. Joining a team of committed educators, Dr. Foley developed a grant proposal to address high school students identified as problem students. Efforts were made to develop a plan to increase the success rate of these students, and a grant was awarded to Palm Beach County providing funds for a "Reluctant Learner" program.

Deemed a success after three years, Dr. Foley went on to accept an invitation to become a professor at Florida Atlantic University, continuing his extensive work in the field of education. He served over thirty years with the Southern Association of Colleges and Schools with the Commission on Secondary Schools. Dr. Foley is the senior author of a secondary school mathematics program published by Addison Wesley.

www.ingramcontent.com/pod-product-compliance
Lightning Source LLC
Chambersburg PA
CBHW030326080526
44584CB00012B/732